Charles Woodruff Shields

Liturgia Expurgata

The Prayer-Book as Amended by the Westminster Divines

Charles Woodruff Shields

Liturgia Expurgata
The Prayer-Book as Amended by the Westminster Divines

ISBN/EAN: 9783337780142

Printed in Europe, USA, Canada, Australia, Japan

Cover: Foto ©Lupo / pixelio.de

More available books at **www.hansebooks.com**

Liturgia Expurgata;

or,

The Prayer-Book

as amended

by the Westminster Divines.

an essay on

The Liturgical Question

in the

American Churches.

by

CHARLES W. SHIELDS, D.D., LL.D.,

professor in princeton college.

FOURTH EDITION.

NEW YORK:
ANSON D. F. RANDOLPH & COMPANY,
900 BROADWAY, COR. 20th STREET.

PREFACE.

The following essay was originally published in connection with the Presbyterian Book of Common Prayer, and properly accompanies that volume as an explanation of the numerous points in which it differs from other editions of the Prayer-Book, though it also contains much matter that is of general and permanent interest.

The suggestion has often been made that it should be issued in this separate form, in order to meet the growing interest that is felt in liturgical, as distinguished from extemporaneous worship, and especially to aid in solving the problem of a liturgy that shall be in accordance with the history, doctrine, and genius of the Presbyterian Church.

The positions maintained in the essay are: that it is now impossible to construct a true liturgy outside of the Prayer-Book, or without regard to the ancient and modern formularies which it contains; and that the Prayer-Book, as amended by the Westminster divines, and made optional rather than obligatory, would supply the need of Presbyterian forms of devotion, for private and public use, and at the same time afford a basis of closer union among the leading Churches of the Reformation (the Lutheran, Reformed, Presbyterian, and Episcopalian), which originally contributed to the formation of the English liturgy.

"There was never anything by the wit of man so well devised, or so sure established, which, in continuance of time, hath not been corrupted: as, among other things, it may plainly appear by the Common Prayers in the Church, commonly called Divine Service."—*Preface to the First Prayer book in* 1549.

"It cannot be thought any disparagement or derogation either to the work itself, or to the compilers of it, or to those who have hitherto used it, if, after more than a hundred years since its first composure, such further emendations be now made therein, as may be judged necessary for satisfying the scruples of a multitude of sober persons, who cannot at all, or very hardly, comply with the use of it, as now it is, and may best suit with the present times after so long an enjoyment of the glorious light of the gospel, and so happy a reformation."—*Preface of the Presbyterian Revisers in* 1661.

"Upon the principles already laid down, it cannot but be supposed that further alterations would in time be found expedient. Accordingly, a commission for a review was issued in the year 1689; but this great and good work miscarried at that time."—*Preface to the American Prayer-book in* 1789.

ADVERTISEMENT.

This Book of Common Prayer is designed, and is believed to be fitted, to promote the following objects:

1. To serve as a memorial of those learned divines of the Westminster Assembly who, as Presbyters and Presbyterians in the Church of England, were, in 1645, the framers of the Directory for Public Worship, and in 1661 the revisers of the Book of Common Prayer.

2. To furnish private members of the Church with a collection of solemn and decorous forms of devotion which have been used by the learned and pious in all ages, and, as here presented, are freed from the peculiarities that render other editions of the Prayer-book unserviceable.

3. To provide a manual of examples and materials of divine service for the use of Pastors, Ministers, Theological Students, Chaplains, and others called to conduct public worship; and also, for the use of any congregations desiring to combine a Liturgy with the Directory, a service-book which, besides every other liturgical merit, has that of expressing the orthodoxy

and resting upon the authority of the framers of the Westminster standards.

4. To increase, beyond our own communion, the spirit of catholicity and fraternity among such Churches of the Reformation as originally contributed to the formation of the Prayer-book, by restoring to more general use those ancient formulas which are their several production or common inheritance, and, next to the Holy Scriptures, the closest visible bond of their unity.

The Supplementary Treatise of the Editor is designed to give the warrant, history, and analysis of all that the Revised Prayer-book contains.

CONTENTS.

CHAPTER I.
The Origin of the Westminster Directory for Public Worship, ... 9

CHAPTER II.
The Presbyterian Revision of the Book of Common Prayer, ... 13

CHAPTER III.
The General Assembly's Revision of the Westminster Directory, ... 22

CHAPTER IV.
Ministerial Neglects, and their Remedies, under the Directory, ... 28

CHAPTER V.
Congregational Neglects, and their Remedies, under the Directory, ... 35

CHAPTER VI.
The Consistency of a Free Liturgy with the Directory, ... 41

CHAPTER VII.

The Warrant for the Presbyterian Book of Common Prayer,... 50

CHAPTER VIII.

The Historical Materials for the Presbyterian Book of Common Prayer,............................. 62

CHAPTER IX.

The Historical and Critical Analysis of the Amended Presbyterian Prayer-book,................... 76

APPENDIX I.

A Chronological List of the Principal Liturgical and Historical Documents connected with the compilation and revision of the Prayer-book, and used in the preparation of this edition,............. 137

APPENDIX II.

The Presbyterian Exceptions against the Book of Common Prayer in 1661, with Notes tracing their previous and subsequent history,.............. 141

APPENDIX III.

A General Index to the Historical Sources of the Offices in the Presbyterian Prayer-book,....... 179

APPENDIX IV.

A Tabular View of the Presbyterian Prayer-book as compared with the Episcopalian, Calvinistic, Lutheran, Mediæval, and Primitive Liturgies, 188

THE
DIRECTORY FOR PUBLIC WORSHIP

AND THE

BOOK OF COMMON PRAYER.

CHAPTER I.

THE ORIGIN OF THE WESTMINSTER DIRECTORY FOR PUBLIC WORSHIP.

It may sometimes happen that Churches will have so far departed, in the progress of events, from their own early standards and usages, that the work of restoration must incur somewhat of the suspicion belonging to that of innovation. In such a case, we have no alternative but to calmly appeal from existing prejudices to facts, authorities, and principles, and then leave the truth to vindicate itself, in the face of any odium or ridicule that may arise.

The writer, therefore, in entering upon the difficult but vital question of this treatise, has but to premise, that the views advocated are believed to be not only scriptural and reasonable, but in accordance with the history and the best interests of the Church to which he belongs; that they are held neither in a sectarian nor in a latitudinarian spirit; that they have not been hastily formed, but are the result of some years of study and experience; and that they are not meant to be here advanced without due caution and deference. It would be too much to expect a ready assent to them on the part of those who have not passed through some similar course of reflection; but it is hoped they will at least be received in the spirit in which they are offered.*

Our first resort must be to that portion of our Church standards, known as the "Directory for Public Worship." This is the more necessary, since but few Presbyterians in this country would seem to be acquainted with its origin, or rightly to appreciate its advantages as a mean between the extremes of imposed liturgies and "irregular, or extravagant effusions" in the service of God; as is abundantly shown by the general neglect into which it has fallen.

In the Scotch editions of the Confession of Faith, the formulary has this title—"The Directory for the Public Worship of God, agreed upon by the Assembly of Divines at Westminster, with the assistance of Commissioners from the Church of Scotland, as a part of the Covenanted uniformity in religion betwixt the Churches of Christ in the kingdoms of Scotland, England, and Ireland." But, as first adopted, and by law established, it was entitled, "A Directory for the Public Worship of God, throughout the three kingdoms of England, Scotland, and Ireland; together with an ordinance of Parliament for the taking away of the Book of Common Prayer, and the Establishing and Observing of this present Directory throughout the Kingdom of England and Dominion of Wales." These titles, viewed in connection with several previous events, will afford a sufficient clue to its origin.

While the Church of Scotland differed from the Church of England, in having been reformed from Popery by presbyters rather than by prelates, it agreed with it, and with all the Reformed Churches, in adhering both to the principle and to the use of a liturgy. The "Book of Common Prayer" itself was, at one time,

---

* While the Editor of the Presbyterian Book of Common Prayer is alone responsible for the manner in which he has performed his task, yet it is proper to state, that he has not acted without consultation with prominent Ministers of our Church, and has had the advantage of suggestions from the late Dr. William M. Engles and Professor Charles Hodge, who separately examined the proof-sheets of the work, while it was passing through the press.

in use in many Presbyterian parishes;* and the "Book of Common Order," at length adopted by the General Assembly, had some things in common with the Prayer Book, as will appear on comparing them. And even the first proposals to introduce the English liturgy into Scotland, were so favorably entertained by the General Assembly, that under its sanction a Prayer Book, substantially agreeing with that of the Church of England, was prepared, though never actually used.†

What might have been the result, had these measures been pursued with moderation and caution by the succeeding king, it were now simply curious to inquire. But the rise of the High Church party in England, under the lead of Archbishop Laud, the revival of many papistical ceremonies in the Church service, and the wild attempt of King Charles I. to impose them by force of arms upon the people of Scotland, soon dashed all hopes of uniformity or conformity in worship between the two kingdoms, on the basis of any existing liturgy. It was enough to rouse the Scots to a frenzy, that the book sent to them was a foreign production, and had not been regularly passed upon by their own Church courts, even if on examination it had been found free from errors and superstitions. The first attempt to use it in the cathedral at Edinburgh, was frustrated by a popular outbreak. "The Service-book, the bishops themselves, and every rag and remnant of Episcopacy, were blown away out of Scotland, to the four winds of heaven, by the first breath of that tempest." And at length all ranks and orders, throughout England as well as Scotland, with a contagious enthusiasm, banded themselves together to resist the invasion, and defend the Reformed religion against the fresh inroad of the old hierarchy. To make this compact more binding and impressive, it was preceded by a public fast, and attended with the religious solemnity of an oath; the

---

* Collier's Ecclesiastical History, vi. 580, vii. 388. Peterkin's Records of the Kirk of Scotland, p. iv. Heylin's History of the Reformation, Vol. II. p. 322. note.

† Collier, vii. 388; Cook's History of the Church of Scotland, Vol. II. p. 336; Calderwood's True History of the Church of Scotland, pp. 5, 663, 715—17; Hall's Reliquiæ Liturgicæ, Vol. I. p. 19.

whole assembly—parliament, divines, and people—rising at the close of the service, and, with uplifted hands, uniting in a "Solemn League and Covenant,"* of which the following was the first article:

"We noblemen, barons, knights, gentlemen, citizens, burgesses, ministers of the gospel, and commons of all sorts, in the kingdoms of Scotland, England, and Ireland, by the providence of God, living under one king, and being of one reformed religion, having before our eyes the glory of God, and the advancement of the kingdom of our Lord and Saviour Jesus Christ, the honor and happines of the king's majesty and his posterity, and the true public liberty, and peace of the kingdoms, wherein every one's private condition is included; and calling to mind the treacherous and bloody plots, conspiracies, attempts and practices of the enemies of God against the true religion and professors thereof in all places, especially in these three kingdoms, ever since the reformation of religion; and how much their rage, power, and presumption are of late, and at this time, increased and exercised, whereof the deplorable state of the Church and kingdom of *Ireland*, the distressed estate of the Church and kingdom of *England*, and the dangerous estate of the Church and kingdom of *Scotland*, are present and public testimonies. We have now at last (after other means of supplication, remonstrance, protestation, and sufferings,) for the preservation of ourselves and our religion from utter ruin and destruction, according to the commendable practice of these kingdoms in former times, and the example of God's people in other nations; after mature deliberation, resolved and determined to enter into a mutual and solemn league and covenant, wherein we all subscribe, and each one of us for himself, with our hands lifted up to the Most High God, do swear,

"I. That we shall sincerely, really, and constantly, through the grace of God, endeavor, in our several places and callings, the preservation of the reformed religion in the Church of Scotland, in doctrine, worship, discipline, and government, against our common enemies; the reformation of religion in the kingdoms of England and Ireland, in doctrine, worship, discipline, and government,

---

* "The Solemn League and Covenant, for Reformation and Defence of Religion, the honor and happiness of the King, and the peace and safety of the three kingdoms of *Scotland*, *England*, and *Ireland*, agreed upon by Commissioners from the Parliament and Assembly of Divines in England, with Commissioners of the Convention of Estates and General Assembly in Scotland; approved by the General Assembly of the Church of *Scotland*, and by both Houses of Parliament and Assembly of Divines in *England*, and taken and subscribed by them, *Anno* 1643; and thereafter by the said authority, taken and subscribed by all ranks in *Scotland* and *England* the same year; and ratified by act of Parliament of *Scotland*, *Anno* 1644. And again renewed in *Scotland*, with an acknowledgment of sins, and engagement to duties, by all ranks. *Anno* 1648, and by the Parliament 1649; and taken and subscribed by King *Charles II.*, at Spey, June 23, 1650; and at Scoon, **January 1, 1651.**"—*Confession of Faith of the Church of Scotland.*

according to the word of God, and the example of the best Reformed Churches; and shall endeavor to bring the churches of God in the three kingdoms to the nearest conjunction and uniformity in religion, Confession of Faith, Form of Church Government, Directory for Worship, and Catechising; that we, and our people after us, may, as brethren, live in faith and love."

It was thus that the Scotch Covenanters, being now in league with the English Puritans, defeated the Prelatical party in the field, and obtained in Parliament the convocation at Westminster, of that famous assembly of divines to which we owe our Directory.

Of this *Magna Charta* of a pure and free worship, it is enough to say, that it has received praise from intelligent adversaries, no less than friends, as a solemn, temperate, and most instructive document; and that, after the lapse of two centuries, it remains among the authorized formularies of the Church of Scotland, and of the kindred Presbyterian Churches of this country. To be rightly judged, however, either as to matter or style, it should only be viewed in its full form, as first set forth by the Westminster divines, and in the light of the political and religious events from which it sprang.

CHAPTER II.

THE PRESBYTERIAN REVISION OF THE BOOK OF COMMON PRAYER AT THE SAVOY CONFERENCE.

THE reign of the Directory in the Church of England was short. The wave which had brought the Presbyterians into power soon overwhelmed them, and their religious reformation was hurried beyond their control into a political revolution. Having thrust down the Episcopalians, they were now, in their turn, thrust down by the Independents, or Congregationalists, and both Directory and Prayer-book sank from view in the confusions which followed.

Out of this anarchy, the Presbyterian clergy rose foremost in restoring order and peace, both to Church and State. In London, they issued a public protest against the murder of the king, and rebuked the excesses of the rebel army;* and in Scotland, they recalled his successor from exile, crowned him, and rallied to his standard, in opposition to Cromwell. And now the strange sight was presented, of Covenanter in arms against Puritan, both fighting and praying in the face of their own mutual and solemn league and covenant.

After a dreary period of defeat and disorder, the result was the reëstablishment of the throne and Constitution. But it by no means followed, that because the Presbyterians had thus been instrumental in restoring the monarchy, they also intended the restoration of that hierarchy which, from the first, had been the only object of their hostility.† Nor did it seem unreasonable that the Church of England, in accordance with the national sentiment, might continue substantially Presbyterian, both in polity and liturgy.‡ The parliament

---

* "A Serious and Faithful Representation of the Judgments of the Ministers of the Gospel within the province of London." See Collier. Eccl. Hist. ix. p. 357.

† "A Defence of our Proposals to his Majesty for Agreement in Matters of Religion." "The Petition of the Ministers to the King upon the First Draft of his Declaration." "Alterations in the Declaration proposed by the Ministers." See *Documents relating to the Settlement of Church of England in* 1662, pp. 39, 79, 98. Published by the United Saint Bartholomew Committee. London, 1862.

‡ "The Presbyterians," says Collier, an Episcopalian historian, "had several circumstances of advantage to support their hopes. Possession of the chair, the inclinations of no small numbers of the people, the countenance of great men, and the king's Declaration at Breda, gave this party no uncomfortable prospect."

"The Presbyterians," says Bishop Burnet, "were possessed of most of the great benefices in the church, chiefly in the city of London, and in the two universities..... There were a great many of them in very eminent posts, *who were legally possessed of them,* and who had gone into the design of the Restoration in so signal a manner, and with such success, that they had great merit," &c. Burnet's History of his Own Times, p. 89.

"They represented," says Bancroft, "a powerful portion of the aristocracy of England; they had, besides the majority in the Commons, the exclusive possession of the House of Lords; they held command of the army, they had numerous and active adherents among the clergy; the English people favored them. Scotland, which had been so efficient in all that had thus far been done, was entirely devoted to their interests, and they hoped for a compromise with their sovereign."

"The Presbyterians," says Neal, who was far from being their

and the aristocracy were then inclined to presbytery, as a safe mean between prelacy and independency. Leading prelates themselves had already favored a "reduction of episcopacy," to be attained by making the diocesan bishop a sort of permanent moderator of presbytery or synod;* and as the Directory had many of the rubrical elements of the Prayer-book, it was not impossible to combine the freedom and spirituality of the former, with the order and decorum of the latter, and thus, while securing their respective advantages, also escape their respective perils.

Accordingly, in the deputation which recalled Charles the Second to the throne, were such leading Presbyterian divines as Drs. Reynolds, Bates, Calamy, Baxter, &c., who presented an address‡ to the king, in which they said:

"We are satisfied in our judgments concerning the lawfulness of a Liturgy, or Form of Public Worship, provided that it be for the matter agreeable unto the Word of God, and fitly suited to the nature of the several ordinances and necessities of the Church; neither too tedious in the whole, nor composed of too short prayers, unmeet repetitions or responsals; nor to be dissonant from the Liturgies of other Reformed Churches; nor too rigorously imposed; nor the minister so confined thereunto, but that he may also make use of those gifts for prayer and exhortation, which Christ hath given him for the service and edification of the Church."

" And inasmuch as the Book of Common Prayer hath in it many things that are justly offensive, and need amendment, hath been long discontinued, and very many, both ministers and people, persons of pious, loyal, and peaceable minds, are therein greatly dissatisfied; whereupon, if it be again imposed, will inevitably follow sad divisions, and widening of the breaches which your Majesty is now endeavoring to heal; we do most humbly offer to your Majesty's wisdom, that for preventing so great evil, and for settling the Church in unity and peace, some learned, godly, and moderate divines, of

---

friend, "were in possession of the whole power of England; the council of State, the chief officers of the army and navy, and the governors of the chief forts and garrisons, were theirs; their clergy were in possession of both universities, and of the best livings of the kingdom." See Hodge's History of the Presbyterian Church, p. 25—27.

* "The Reduction of Episcopacy unto the form of Synodical Government." See Document V., and Bayne's Historical Introduction to the Documents, p. 106. Also Calamy's Life of Baxter, chap. viii; and Knox's Book of Common Order

‡ "The First Address and Proposals of the Ministers." See Documents relating to the settlement of the Church of England by the Act of Uniformity, in 1662, p. 12.

both persuasions, indifferently chosen, may be employed to compile such a form as is before described, as much as may be in Scripture words: or at least to revise and effectually reform the old, together with an addition or insertion of some other varying forms in Scripture phrase, to be used at the minister's choice; of which variety and liberty there be instances in the Book of Common Prayer."

And the result of this application was "his Majesty's Declaration to all his loving subjects concerning Ecclesiastical Affairs,"* wherein, among other pledges given for a proper fusion of episcopacy with presbytery in the Church, was this one concerning the proposed revision of the Prayer-book:

"Since we find some exceptions made against several things therein, we will appoint an equal number of learned divines, of both persuasions, to review the same, and to make such alterations as shall be thought most necessary, and some additional forms, (in the Scripture phrase as near as may be,) uited unto the several parts of worship, and that it be le. ɔ the minister's choice to use one or other at his discretion."

For the assurances given in this Royal Declaration, the Presbyterian clergy of London presented an "Humble and Grateful Acknowledgement"† to the King, who, at the same time, appointed several of them his chaplains, while to others were offered high preferments, none of which, however, were accepted but the bishopric of Norwich, by Dr. Reynolds, and that only on the conditions of the Declaration.‡ And at length, in due

---

* See Documents, &c., p. 63; Cardwell's History of Conferences on Prayer-book, p. 256.

† See Documents, &c., p. 101, and Reliquiæ Baxterianæ, by Sylvester, p 284.

‡ Calamy's Life of Baxter, p. 155; Hume's History of England, p. 478, Harper's edition; Proctor's History of Prayer-book, p. 114; Non-Conformists' Memorial, vol. i. p. 24; Neal's History of the Puritans, vol. ii. 216. Bishop Reynolds had been a prominent member of the Westminster Assembly, and was not only appointed, but acted on the side of the Presbyterian divines in the Savoy Conference. Baxter says that he "persuaded him to acccept the bishopric." Reid attributes his continuance in it to "a covetous and politic consort." Calamy says that "he carried the wounds of the Church with him to his grave;" and Neal that he was "a frequent preacher, a constant resident in his diocese, and a good old Puritan, who never concerned himself with the politics of the court." He is termed, by different writers, "the pride and glory of the Presbyterians in the city of London," "one of the most eloquent preachers of his age," a "thorough Calvinist," and a "strenuous opposor of the *jus divinum* of episcopacy."

form, a commission was issued for the promised revision to twelve Episcopalian divines, with nine coadjutors, and likewise to as many, the following named, Presbyterian divines, then incumbents of various livings:

PRESBYTERIAN COMMISSIONERS AT THE SAVOY CONFERENCE, A. D. 1661.

Principals.

ANTHONY TUCKNEY, D. D.,
    Regius Prof. of Div., Cambridge.
JOHN CONANT, D. D.,
    Regius Prof. of Div., Oxford.
WILLIAM SPURSTOW, D. D.,
    Mast. Katharine Hall, Cambridge.
JOHN WALLIS, D. D.,
    Sav. Prof. of Geometry, Oxford.
THOMAS MANTON, D. D.,
    St. Paul's, London.
EDMUND CALAMY, D. D.,
    Perp. Cur. of Aldermanbury.
Rev. RICHARD BAXTER.
    Minister at Kidderminster.
Rev. ARTHUR JACKSON,
    St. Faith's, London.
Rev. THOMAS CASE,
    St. Mary Magdalen, London.
Rev. SAMUEL CLARKE,
    Perp Cur. Bennet Fink, London.
Rev. MATTHEW NEWCOMEN,
    Vicar of Dedham.
EDWARD REYNOLDS, D. D.,
    Bishop of Norwich.

Coadjutors.

THOMAS HORTON, D. D.,
    Prof. of Div., Gresh. Col., Cambridge.
THOMAS JACOMB, D. D.,
    St. Martin's, London.
WILLIAM BATES, D. D.,
    St. Dunstan's, London.
WILLIAM COOPER, D. D.,
    St. Olave, London.
Rev. JOHN RAWLINSON,
    Vicar of Lambeth.
JOHN LIGHTFOOT, D. D.,
    Vice Chancellor of Cambridge.
JOHN COLLINS, D. D.,
    St. Stephens, Norwich.
BENJAMIN WOODBRIDGE, D. D.,
    Vicar of Newbury.
ROGER DRAKE, D. D.,
    St. Peter's, London.

The terms of the Commission ran thus:

"Charles the Second, by the grace of God, King of England, Scotland, France, and Ireland, defender of the faith, &c. To our trusty and well-beloved the most reverend father in God Accepted archbishop of York, the right reverend fathers in God Gilbert bishop of London, John bishop of Durham, John bishop of Rochester, Henry bishop of Chichester, Humphrey bishop of Sarum. George bishop of Worcester, Robert bishop of Lincoln, Benjamin bishop of Peterborough, Bryan bishop of Chester, Richard bishop of Carlisle, John bishop of Exeter, Edward bishop of Norwich; and to our trusty and well-beloved the reverend Anthony Tuckney Dr. in divinity, John Conant Dr in divinity, William Spurstow Dr. in divinity, John Wallis Dr. in divinity, Thomas Manton Dr. in divinity, Edmund Calamy batchelor in divinity, Richard Baxter clerk, Arthur Jackson clerk, Thomas Case, Samuel Clark, Matthew Newcomen clerks: and to our trusty and well-beloved Dr. Earles dean of Westminster, Peter Heylen Dr. in divinity, John Hacket Dr. in divinity, John Barwick Dr. in divinity, Peter Gunning Dr. in divinity, John Pearson Dr. in divinity, Thomas Pierce Dr. in divinity, Anthony Sparrow Dr. in divinity, Herbert Thorndike batchelor in divinity, Thomas Horton Dr. in divinity, Thomas Jacomb Dr. in divinity, William Bates, John Rawlinson clerks, William Cooper clerk, Dr. John Lightfoot, Dr. John Collinges, Dr. Benjamin Woodbridge, and William Drake clerk, greeting. Whereas by our Declaration of the five and twentieth of October last concerning ecclesiastical affairs, we did amongst other things express our esteem of the liturgy of the Church of England, contained in the Book of Common Prayer; and yet since we find some exceptions made against several things therein, we did by our said Declaration declare we would appoint an equal number of learned divines of both persuasions, to review the same, and to make such alterations therein as should be thought most necessary, and some additional forms in the Scripture phrase, as near as might be, suited unto the nature of the several parts of pub'ic worship: we therefore in accomplishment of our said will and intent, and of our continued and constant care and study for the peace and unity of the Churches within our dominions, and for the removal of all exceptions and differences, and the occasions of such differences and exceptions from amongst our good subjects, for or concerning the said Book of Common Prayer, or any thing therein contained, do by these our letters patent require, authorize, constitute and appoint you the said archbishop, bishops, doctors, and persons, to advise upon and review the said Book of Common Prayer, comparing the same with the most ancient liturgies which have been used in the church, in the primitive and purest times: and to that end to assemble and meet together from time to time, and at such times within the space of four calendar months now next ensuing, in the master's lodging in the Savoy in the Strand, in the county of Middlesex, or in such other place, or places, as to you shall be thought fit and convenient, to take into your serious and grave consideration, the several directions and rules, forms of prayer, and things in the said Book of Common Prayer contained, and to advise, and consult upon and about the same, and the several exceptions and objections which shall now be raised against the same. And if occasion be, to make such reasonable and necessary alterations, correc tions and amendments therein, as by and between you the said archbishop, bishops, doctors, and persons hereby required to meet and advize, as aforesaid, shall be agreed upon to be needful or expedient for the giving satisfaction to tender consciences, and the restoring and continuance of peace and unity, in the churches under our protection and government; but avoiding as much as may be, all unnecessary alterations of the forms and liturgy wherewith the people are already acquainted, and have so long received in the Church of England."*

It will be found, on comparing this document with the King's Declaration, that meanwhile the parties had materially changed ground. So that no sooner were they confronted, than it was made plain they were to enter upon "a campaign rather than a conference." The Episcopalians stiffly assumed the defensive, insisted upon the formality of a written debate,† and demanded a list of objections; and the Presbyterians finding, after a lengthy correspondence, ending in a mere logical wrangle, that no terms could be made with them, withdrew at last, in hope of holding the King to his pledges,‡ and obtaining redress in Parliament. A renewed appeal, drawn up by Baxter, concluded in these words:

"Finally, as your Majesty, under God, is the protection whereto your people fly, and as the same necessities still remain which drew forth your gracious Declaration, we most humbly and earnestly beseech your Majesty that the benefits of the said Declaration may be continued to your people; and, in particular, that none be punished or troubled for not using the Common Prayer, until it be effectually reformed, and the additions made that are therein expressed. We crave your Majesty's pardon for the tediousness of this address, and shall wait in hope that so great a calamity to your people, as would follow the loss of so many able, faithful ministers, as rigorous impositions would cast out, shall never be recorded in the history of your reign; but that these impediments of concord being forborne, your kingdoms may flourish in piety and peace."§

But in this hope they were doomed to be disappointed.

---

* "The King's Warrant for the Conference at the Savoy." See Document XIV.

† This manœuvre, though it had the effect, at the time, of placing the Presbyterian commissioners in a false position, has, however, secured to us, as we shall see, the full records of the Conference.

‡ See "Efforts of Presbyterian Ministers to have the King's Declaration of October 1660, enacted." Document XXV.

§ "The due Account and humble Petition of us Ministers of the Gospel, lately commissioned for the Review and Alteration of the Liturgy." Document XXIII.

The vaunted "word of a king" proved but a broken reed; and with the duplicity* of Charles, and the servility of Parliament, were thrown against them all the libellous† influences in which that corrupt age abounded. The Prayer-book, with its exceptionable features unchanged, was presented to the House of Commons; and at length, by the close vote of 186 to 180, the House of Lords reluctantly assenting,‡ was passed that famous "Act of Uniformity," under the operation of which, on St. Bartholomew's Day, (now doubly memorable in our annals,) two thousand Presbyterian clergy, then unsurpassed in learning, loyalty, or piety, and comprising names whose praise is still in all the churches, chose rather to quit their livings, in the face of beggary and disgrace, than continue in an establishment unto which they could not conscientiously conform.§ And, at the

---

* "I must tell you," said the king, in one of his speeches to the Commons, "I have the worst luck in the world, if, after all the reproaches of being a papist, whilst I was abroad, I am suspected of being a Presbyterian, now I am come home." Journals of Parliament relating to the Act of Uniformity. Document XXVI. See also Bishop Burnet's History of his Own Time, pp. 92, 179.

† Burnet, p. 184, and Neal, vol ii. p. 217.

‡ Knight's History of England, Book VIII., p. 801.

§ "St. Bartholomew's day being come, on which the Act of Uniformity was to take place, two thousand Presbyterian ministers chose rather to quit their livings than to subscribe to the conditions of this Act. It was expected that a division would have happened amongst them, and that a great number of them would have chose rather to conform to the Church of England than to see themselves reduced to beggary. It was not, therefore, without extreme surprise that they were all seen to stand out,—not so much as one suffering himself to be tempted. As this is a considerable event of this reign, it will not be improper to inquire into the causes of this rigor against the Presbyterians." Rapin's History of England, as quoted in Collier, ix. 453.

"On one and the same day, England saw the becoming spectacle of two thousand ministers of Jesus Christ embracing penury rather than stoop to dishonest compliance. From college halls and cathedral closes, from stately and from humble parsonages, endeared by the familiarity of happy and useful years; holy men led out their delicately nurtured families, not knowing whither they should go." Palfry's History of New England, vol. ii. p. 130.

"It is not this or that thing that puts us upon this dissent," said Jacomb, of St. Martin's, Ludgate, "but it is *conscience towards God* and fear of offending Him. I censure none that differ from me, as though they displease God; but yet, as to myself, should I do thus and thus, I should certainly violate the peace of my own conscience, and offend God, which I must not do. Shall we not follow those

same time, by one of those astounding revolutions with which history sometimes sets all philosophy at defiance, Episcopacy was established in Scotland on the ruins of the Covenant and Directory.

And thus it seemed that every vestige of Protestant liberty had been swept out of the three kingdoms. The event proved, however, that it was but a brief recoil, as if to collect strength for a last triumphant effort. In the year 1690, in the reign of the Calvinistic King William, Presbytery again rose from under the heel of Prelacy, and achieved, in the Church of Scotland, such a legal establishment as had before extinguished it in the Church of England. The Directory and the Prayer-book were driven farther apart than ever, and the two extremities of the island settled down into those extremes of Protestant churchmanship in which they have continued until the present day.*

---

who, through faith and patience, inherit the promises? Shall we leave the snow of Lebanon for Kedar and Meschech? No! let us commit ourselves to the care of our Heavenly Father. Arise! let us go hence!" Quoted in New Englander, Jan. 1863.

* It will be seen that, in this chapter, we have given only so much of the history of the times as directly bears upon the present investigation. It was confessedly an age of intolerance when both parties by turns became persecutors and victims; and we have not thought it necessary to enter into controversies so remote from our time and country; if indeed we are not spared the necessity of vindicating that comparatively lenient Presbyterian rule of which Jeremy Taylor (while allowed to pursue the vocation of a teacher in Wales) could speak as "the gentleness and mercy of a noble enemy." Our aim has not been to paint either party as tyrants or saints; but simply to bring to view the unquestionable fact that the framers of our Church standards were not only, at the time, as a body, the lawful inheritors of the Prayer-book, but also that they afterwards, by their own action, became its lawful revisers, with a view to its resumption. The case was different with the Independent or Congregational ministers, who, from disloyalty, as well as doctrinal repugnance, forfeited their livings; but the incumbency of the Presbyterian clergy, together with that of the ejected Episcopalians, was placed beyond question by the Act 12, Car. ii. cap. 17, entitled "An Act for *confirming* and *restoring* of ministers;" and when it is remembered that the whole number of claimants for *restoration* was not above two or three hundred, we shall know how to estimate the wild assertion sometimes made, that seven thousand or eight thousand Episcopalian martyrs are to be weighed against the two thousand Presbyterians. See Calamy's Account and Remarks on Dr. Walker's Account, vols. i. and ii. Consult also Burnet and Neal, and the civil historians, Hume, Hallam, Macaulay, Knight, and May.

CHAPTER III.

THE GENERAL ASSEMBLY'S REVISION OF THE WESTMINSTER DIRECTORY FOR PUBLIC WORSHIP.

Our historical sketch (in which we have aimed at truth and fairness) has brought to view these facts: 1st. That liturgies, or prescribed forms of public worship, were in use in the early Church of Scotland, as in all the Reformed Churches; 2d. That the Directory was, in its origin, a revolutionary protest against civil and ecclesiastical tyranny in such matters, and a concession to the principle of uniformity or conformity peculiar to established or State-religions;* 3d. That it was followed by a healthy reaction—there having been at one time at least two thousand Presbyterian clergy in England who would have been willing to use even the Prayer-book itself, had it been properly reformed and amended; and 4th. That the Directory was finally established by law in Scotland, as the alternative to a legally imposed liturgy, and as the only existing safeguard of a free and spiritual worship.

We come now to its history in our own country. It was certainly not necessary that these extremes, between which the Church was driven in the Old World, should have been repeated on a larger scale in the New, necessitated, as they mainly were, by political and sectarian controversies, which no longer trammel us on this side of the Atlantic; and it is not even probable that they would have been so repeated, had our fathers been able to free themselves from inherited prejudices, and to foresee the present diversified condition and rela-

---

* These points are fully proved in the two learned and valuable works of Rev. Charles W. Baird, to whom belongs the credit of a first investigator and collector of the Presbyterian Liturgies. "Eutaxia, or the Presbyterian Liturgies; Historical Sketches by a Minister of the Presbyterian Church," published by M. W. Dod; and "A Book of Public Prayer, compiled from the authorized formularies of the Presbyterian Church, as prepared by the Reformers, Calvin, Knox, Bucer, and others, with Supplementary Forms. Published by Charles Scribner, 1857.

tions of our Church. As it was, it is well known that in the General Assembly which adopted our Confession of Faith, the most learned and judicious members, such as Drs. Rogers, McWhorter, Ashbel Green, were in favor of so enlarging the liturgical element of the Directory, as to include in it not merely rules and topics, but complete forms for the minister's use, either as examples or materials of divine service; and the committee of revision actually prepared and reported such a liturgy, and advocated its adoption.* The failure of the scheme is not now to be wondered at, or indeed, regretted; especially since the spirit which prompted it so far prevailed in the counsels of the Assembly as to procure the amendment of the Directory in several particulars. We shall see, if we compare our edition of that formulary with the same as first adopted by the Westminster divines, that the *additions* we have made to it are decidedly liturgical in their tendency.

In the chapter on the "Preaching of the Word," we find added this much needed caution against the danger of degrading public worship into mere sermonizing:

"As one primary design of public ordinances is to pay social acts of homage to the *Most High God*, ministers ought to be careful not to make their sermons so long as to interfere with or exclude the more important duties of prayer and praise; but preserve a just proportion between the several parts of public worship."

In the chapter on the "Singing of Psalms" and hymns, (which latter compositions† are not named in the Westminster formulary,) it is recommended to congregations "to cultivate some knowledge of the rules of music, that we may praise God in a becoming manner with our voices, as well as with our hearts;" and to ministers, "that more time be allowed for this excellent part of divine service than has been usual in most of our churches."

---

* Assembly's Digest, p. 9. Eutaxia, or the Presbyterian Liturgies, Chap xiii

† The history of our present *Hymn Book* affords some instructive precedents in reference to the corresponding question of a *Prayer Book*, and shows how steadily the reaction has been going on in modern Presbyterianism, from that false extreme into which it was driven in the Church of Scotland. Assembly's Digest—Psalmody, pp. 180—187.

The chapter on "Public Prayer" is made more exact and methodical, the matter of such devotions being placed under several heads, as *Adorations, Thanksgivings, Confessions, Supplications, Pleadings,* and *Intercessions;* while, as to the manner, the use of forms is neither enjoined nor forbidden, as appears from this important amendment:

"We think it necessary to observe, that although we do not approve, as is well known, of confining ministers to set or fixed forms of prayer for public worship, yet it is the indispensable duty of every minister, previously to his entering on his office, to prepare and qualify himself for this part of his duty, as well as for preaching. He ought, by a thorough acquaintance with the Holy Scriptures, by reading the best writers on the subject, by meditation, and by a life of communion with God in secret, to endeavor to acquire both the spirit and the gift of prayer. Not only so, but when he is to enter on particular acts of worship, he should endeavor to compose his spirit, and to digest his thoughts for prayer, that it may be performed with dignity and propriety, as well as to the profit of those who join in it; and that he may not disgrace that important service by mean, irregular, or extravagant effusions."

The entire chapter on "Admission to Sealing Ordinances" is an addition, and thus extracts the kernel of truth from the error of Confirmation:

"Children born within the pale of the visible Church, and dedicated to God in baptism, are under the inspection and government of the Church, and are to be taught to read and repeat the Catechism, the Apostles' Creed, and the Lord's Prayer. They are to be taught to pray, to abhor sin, to fear God, and to obey the Lord Jesus Christ. And, when they come to years of discretion, if they be free from scandal, appear sober and steady, and have sufficient knowledge to discern the Lord's body, they ought to be informed it is their duty and privilege to come to the Lord's Supper."

While such significant additions as these are to be noticed, it is still to be regretted that the suggestions in reference to the reading of the Scriptures and of the Psalms, should not have been more fully retained, and that the specific direction as to the use of the Lord's Prayer should have been inconsistently (see Larger Catechism, Q 187,) and no doubt inadvertently, omitted.

The Directory, as thus amended at its adoption, has remained, without material alteration, our authorized guide in public worship; but the spirit which ruled in those amendments has continued in various ways to express itself. The insertion of that form in our hymn books, designed for use in divine service; the issue by our Board, of such manuals as "Miller on Public Prayer," the "Sailor's Companion, or, Book of Public and Private Devotions for Seamen;" and the publication of such works as "Eutaxia, or the Presbyterian Liturgies," and "A Book of Public Prayer, Compiled from the Authorized Formularies of the Presbyterian Church," are marks of a growing opinion in this matter;* to which may be added the more practical experiment of the "St. Peter's Church," at Rochester.

Even in the mother Church of Scotland, on the very battle-ground of the Directory, the Moderator of the General Assembly, in his opening sermon,† has recommended and ably advocated a more liturgical mode of

---

* See also Princeton Review, 1855, Art. V., "Presbyterian Liturgies;" and 1847, Art. IV., "Public Prayer." The author of the last named article speaks of having "sometimes heard the intimation, that the Book of Common Prayer, could it be quietly introduced, would be an improvement upon the present forms of devotion in many of our pulpits."

† He explains that there are many who "are dissatisfied, not with our doctrine, but with our external forms of worship. The complaint is, that our services are bald and cold; that they are ill-fitted to evoke the feelings and emotions which become worshippers; that we come together rather as an audience to hear a lecturer or teacher, than to pour forth our confessions, and desires, and prayers for mercy and forgiveness through the blood of Christ; that when prayer is made, it is rather that of presiding ministers than of the assembled people; that they are wholly at the discretion of one man, however mediocre may be his gifts; that this is in no reasonable sense common prayer, for that they often toil after him in vain; that through our present system they are made passive and silent, rather than living worshippers; and are not called to confess within the sanctuary the Lord Jesus with the mouth, though it be written, 'With the heart man believeth unto righteousness, and with the mouth confession is made unto salvation.' . . . . The regulation of these different matters, if there is truth in ecclesiastical history, was, at one period at least, left to congregations and their pastors and rulers; and to them it is humbly submitted, this Church might commit such power with greater security than any other, inasmuch as if any attempt was made to return to the forms and usages of a better age, against the mind of a major part of the congregation, or even to the offending of the honest prepossessions of a considerable portion of it, we have, through the subordination of our judicatories, ample means of granting redress."

He adds: "Many clergymen and members of the Church of Scotland, not the least in name, acquirements, and worth, have frequently discussed the matter with me, and have arrived at the same conclusion."

worship, as essential to the preservation and extension of the Church in some communities. And if we choose to look around us, we shall see on every side sister Churches and denominations, occupied with the problem of a liturgy that shall retain all that is valuable in the Church of the past, and yet be adapted to the Church of the present and the future.

But the general inference we would now draw from the facts before us, is, that there has always been, throughout our history, what may be called a liturgical type or phase of Presbyterianism, and that its advocates are of unimpeachable orthodoxy and piety; being so attached to our Directory as the only safe universal guide for the whole Church, that they "do not approve of confining" pastors or congregations to liturgies, and yet maintaining a voluntary and judicious use of them, in cases where it is plainly needed and desired, to be not only consistent with our standards, but part of that liberty wherewith Christ hath made his people free. And if it be asked why so little practical success has hitherto sanctioned their views, we need only mention two reasons as sufficient to account for past failures.

One fatal mistake has been that of attempting to *compose*, rather than simply to *compile*, a liturgy. Some of the Presbyterian Commissioners to the Savoy Conference, through the injudicious zeal of Baxter, for the addition to the Prayer Book of his "Reformed Liturgy," a hasty effusion of his own, were betrayed into an error, which was most adroitly turned against them by their adversaries;* and our first Assembly's Committee of Revision were on the same path, when they recommended the whole Church, though only as a sample, an entirely new devotional production, ignoring even the hallowed formularies of Calvin and Knox. Scarcely less questionable is our Church pride and sensitiveness sometimes shown in reference to the Prayer Book, as if that excellent compilation, so largely referable to Presbyterian sources and sanctions, were an exclusively Episcopalian production, or as if it were needful to repudiate the common treasury of Christian devotion

---

* Bishop Burnet's History of his own Times, Vol. I., p. 180.

from which much of it was taken. If we intend to act upon this principle in our public worship, we must winnow out of our Hymn Book its Roman Catholic, Episcopalian, and Methodist hymns, and restrict ourselves to Presbyterian poems, set to Presbyterian airs. And the reformation will not be complete until we have banished the organ and the choir from our churches, and succeeded in devising for ourselves an architecture, less heathen or more Protestant than the Greek or Gothic temples in which some of our congregations are content to worship. The truth is, that, strictly speaking, a liturgy, like a creed or confession, cannot be the product of any one mind or age, or even sect of the Church; and it is no wonder that good sense and good taste have always combined with true piety in eschewing forms of worship, whether prescribed or extemporaneous, which are full of individual conceits and ingenious novelties.

But the other, and not less serious, mistake which has been made, is that of hoping to impose, or in any way introduce a liturgy throughout the entire Church, without regard to its diversified condition. We have seen that our whole history is a protest against the interference of the civil power in such matters; many things in the Prayer-book which were simply indifferent, or even laudable, having been resisted to the utmost, when by law enjoined as terms of communion; and the same instinct of liberty rises against any abuse of even Church power in the details of public worship. The genius of presbytery, the world over, cannot endure anything more stringent than a Directory, or system of general rules and suggestions; and to picture her vast communion, ministers and congregations, servilely drilled through the manual of an imposed ritual, would be the wildest of fancies. It may be questioned, indeed, whether the best liturgy that could be framed, were it abruptly taken up and enforced by ecclesiastical authority, would be, if warrantable, on any account desirable. Our Church, as a Church, might find in such appliances a hinderance to her own growth, efficiency, and spirituality; as is shown by the fact, that the denomination which adheres to an im posed liturgy cannot take it effectively outside of the cities, into the country, or to the frontiers. Moreover, in a land so vast and varied as ours, anything like strict uniformity of worship is, in the nature of things, unattainable. It is unreasonable that a congregation in St. Louis or New York should have all its appliances of devotion exactly like those of a congregation in the interior of Pennsylvania, or of Kansas, and such a rigid correspondence does not, in fact, exist throughout our bounds. The Church has, therefore, wisely foreborne either to enjoin or to forbid choirs, organs, particular styles of architecture and furniture, or a stated order and form of the several parts of public worship; and it may be safely assumed that all parties would unite in deprecating any summary legislation in reference to such questions, as not only unnecessary, but an invasion of that constitutional liberty in things indifferent, which we prize as second only to our uniformity in things essential.

In several following chapters we propose to discuss the existing abuses of our Directory, or the evils which have arisen under it, and the available remedies and improvements.

CHAPTER IV.

MINISTERIAL NEGLECTS, AND THEIR REMEDIES UNDER THE DIRECTORY.

IN public worship, the two human parties are the minister and the congregation—the former leading in the service, and the latter accompanying him with the heart, or in some parts, with the voice also; and, for the guidance of these two parties, the Directory gives certain general rules and suggestions. Let us consider, in this article, the ministerial requisites of edifying worship; and we would do this in no censorious or critical spirit, but only out of love to that Church which is the mother of us all, and from a conviction that the defects in our present practice are already generally admitted and regretted, and all the more readily, because they are not past remedy. The writer, indeed, is simply confessing for himself, as well as for others.

And let it be candidly asked, at the outset, if our ministry have not, as a body, widely departed from the direction that "one primary design of public ordinances is to pay social acts of homage to the *Most High God;*" and if, in yielding to the popular taste for able and eloquent sermons, they are not neglecting the prescribed general and special preparation "for this part of their duty as well as for preaching?" No true Presbyterian, indeed, would wish to see the pulpit thrust aside in our worship. It is the glory of Protestant, as it was of primitive Christianity; and our Church, in so carefully furnishing herself with a race of educated preachers and scholars, has acquired a hold upon the intellectual classes, as distinguished from the merely fashionable, or the merely vulgar, which makes her the bulwark of all conservatism throughout the land. But while we have thus signally escaped the evil which existed when, according to the Westminster divines,* "the reading of common prayer was made no better than an idol by many ignorant and superstitious people, who, pleasing themselves in their presence at that service, and their lip-labor in bearing a part in it, have thereby hardened themselves in their ignorance and carelessness of true knowledge and saving piety," may we not meanwhile have lapsed towards the opposite error, of making no better than an idol the reading of a sermon, by so allowing it to "exclude or interfere with the more important duties of prayer and praise,"† that they are degraded into a mere hasty prelude of the preacher, or "disgraced with mean, irregular, or extravagant effusions"?

Some eminent exceptions, indeed, there are to this general neglect: but it cannot be denied that in too many cases there is neither "a just proportion between the several parts of public worship,"† nor any evidence of the required carefulness that they "may be per-

---

* Preface to the Westminster Directory.
† Directory, chap. vi. and chap. v.

formed with dignity and propriety, as well as to the profit of those who join in them."* The matter, form, and arrangement of them have been left to chance or impulse The psalms, hymns, and Scripture readings, or lessons, are selected at random, or upon no obvious principle; and the prayers are long and rambling effusions of what happens to come uppermost in the mind. All is vague, crude, and unedifying; and the congregation, sympathizing with the preacher, are glad to despatch their devotions and come to the sermon, where they can have something more orderly and intelligible.

It is, indeed, often urged, in extenuation of these evils, that worshippers are, or ought to be, in a less critical mood during the devotional than the more didactic part of the service, and certain texts are quoted in favor of the minister's literally taking no thought what shall be said, and relying upon the Holy Spirit absolutely for good utterance, as well as right feeling. It would be easy to parry such texts, and to quote counter-texts;—"God is not the author of confusion in the churches of his saints;" "I will pray with the Spirit, and I will pray with the understanding also;" "Let all things be done decently and in order;" or to cite that methodical form of devotion, combining both directory and liturgy, which our Lord taught his disciples. But we admit the general principle asserted, while we still insist upon its proper limitations. The most acceptable and edifying public worship is, unquestionably, that in which the minister's form and the people's feeling are directly prompted by the Holy Ghost; and yet what shall be said of that in which the form does not fully express the feeling, but in many ways positively thwarts or destroys it—in which there is no well-ordered system of hymns, psalms, lessons, and prayers, by which to excite, sustain, and guide devotion; and in which the worshipper is either driven from public into private prayer, or rendered the worst of formalists? The late Dr. Miller, in his work upon this subject,† has enumerated many, but by no means all, of the defective

---

* Directory, chap. vi. and v.
† Miller on Public Prayer, chap. iv.

forms or modes of public prayer, such as the *repetitious*, the *tedious*, the *irreverent*, the *incoherent*, the *unseasonable*, the *political*, the *complimentary*, the *didactic*, the *rhetorical*, the *sarcastic*, &c. We ask, in all Christian candor, if it is not a gross abuse of the doctrine of spiritual gifts and influences, to rank such effusions as utterances of the Holy Ghost, or to impose them upon a worshipping assembly as *their* prayers? They are not theirs, and cannot be made theirs, any farther than they actually express the desires of their hearts, and are, on their part, intelligently and devoutly offered up unto God.

And this great and growing neglect is already telling injuriously upon our whole system. We believe we only utter a common sentiment, when we say that, on the one hand, it has increased the taste for a style of "sensational" preaching which but few ministers can acquire or sustain; and, on the other hand, has rendered all public prayer and praise a mere foil to the sermon. The pulpit has become the rival of the rostrum, and mere intellectual entertainment substituted for devout communion with God. The people take refuge from the service in the discourse, and the discourse is elaborated at the expense of the service. Whereas, the need of careful preparation for the one only exceeds that for the other by as much as what is offered in the form of prayer or praise to God, is more momentous than what is addressed in the form of mere argument or appeal to man.

Now, the obvious remedy for these evils is to have some plan or method of preparing and conducting the several parts of public worship, by means of which the whole service shall be made at least coherent and intelligible. With most ministers, the only plan would seem to be to adopt the lessons, hymns, and prayers mainly to the sermon. But, while this may be convenient, it can scarcely be called reasonable; for, unless his subject has been before announced, or the occasion itself is suggestive, the congregation are left to grope after him, vaguely guessing his meaning, or else to worship without any intelligent sympathy with him, or with one another. Leaving this principle to be adopted when circumstances require it, a better method, we suggest, would be ordinarily to frame the services before the discourse, entirely independent of it, or at least to have some obvious system in which the sermon shall follow as part of the worship, and not the worship precede as a mere vague prologue to the sermon. The reason for this is, that there are certain "social acts of homage," which every congregation, on ordinary occasions, ought to offer, whatever may be the particular theme the preacher has chosen. Besides his special instruction, there are acts of confession, supplication, intercession, thanksgiving, praise, and hearing of God's word, which must be suited to the various classes, states, and characters of a mixed assembly, and without which their service cannot be called public worship. And to say that every minister can properly express and conduct these varied devotions without any plan or forethought, is to say what every minister knows to be simply impossible. It is for the want of such plan and forethought that large portions of the Scriptures are never read in our churches; that there is scarcely ever a complete service in which no part is slighted or exaggerated, and no class of worshippers neglected, and that in general the ministrations of each pastor are of necessity so impresssed with his own individuality, that the people neither receive from God his whole Word, nor can publicly offer to God their whole heart. And though we would not have the ministry, as a body, come under the bondage of an inflexible system, yet we see no reason why any minister might not for himself so systematize the ordinary church service as to secure at once his own convenience and profit, and the edification of his fellow-worshippers. The leading features of such a system may be briefly indicated as follows:

1. He might arrange a yearly course of Scripture lessons for the instruction of the people in the entire word of God, by reading in every service from both Testaments (according to the suggestion of the original Directory,) not necessarily whole chapters, (which divisions are not inspired, and are often too lengthy for a single reading,) but brief portions, selected in the order of the sacred books themselves, or upon some

other scriptural and rational principle. As Christ is the end and sum of both dispensations, there could be no more effective mode of unfolding the whole divine revelation than that of converging, Sabbath after Sabbath, the blended light of *history* and *prophecy*, of *gospel* and *epistle*, upon the leading events of his life, and the main features of his doctrine. And these lessons might be separated or followed by a *prayer* or *hymn*, in keeping with them, or suited to give devotional expression to them. Such an arrangement, besides imparting variety and unity to the service, would also afford that much-needed relief and help, a stated supply of themes for the sermon.

2. He might adhere to some simple method in the stated public prayers, by at least keeping each class of them distinct and proportionate, so that neither the *confessions*, nor *supplications*, nor *intercessions*, nor *thanksgivings* of the congregation should be omitted, nor "the whole rendered too short or too tedious." The Directory further recommends, besides the cultivation of personal piety, pre-arrangement and pre-meditation as to the matter of such devotions; but whether as to the form of them, there should be anything like composition or compilation from the Scriptures, and the best models, is not decided, and cannot be, by any general rule. "Let every man be fully persuaded in his own mind." It is certain, that the public prayers of some of the holiest and most gifted ministers, such as Drs. Green and Chalmers, were often as carefully prepared as their sermons; and it is equally certain, that the ministrations of other eminent preachers would have been greatly improved by such preparation. Those who most oppose it, are generally those who most need it. There is much ignorant prejudice in reference to this grave matter. Because the warm, unstudied effusions of a good man, evidently in communion with God, and himself as remarkable for prudence as for piety, are confessedly better than the most sincere recitation, and infinitely better than the mere formal reading of prayers, we absurdly elevate the rare exception into a rule. But there is no practical evidence in our ministry to support the specious pretension; and until the

preacher has given proof of an apostolic gift of utterance, it is surely questionable whether he ought to leave his fellow-worshippers wholly at the mercy of his moods and caprices.

3. He might arrange the several parts of worship in some natural order or succession, by which the worshipper should be conducted from the simple to the more difficult and intimate stages of devotion; beginning with an Invocation, or act of Humiliation and Confession, and thence proceeding to the Reading of the Law and the Gospel, with Confession of Faith, through the Supplications and Intercessions, to the crowning acts of Thanksgiving and Praise. And sometimes might be used with profit those excellent summaries of these several parts of public service, the *Commandments*, the *Beatitudes*, the *Apostles' Creed*, the *Lord's Prayer*, and that well-digested series of petitions contained in the reformed *Litany*, the whole being preceded by one of the reformed *Confessions*.

4. He might both have and use a form in those ceremonial offices, for which the Directory provides only general rules, but which cannot, in the nature of the case, be wholly extemporized—such as the "Administration of Baptism," "Administration of the Lord's Supper," "Admission of Persons to Sealing Ordinances," "Solemnization of Marriage," "Burial of the Dead," &c. It is matter of general complaint, if not loud, yet deep, that these solemn occasions are so often marred by crude and random effusions. If only a few well-chosen sentences of Scripture were pronounced at such times, it would be far better than the mere desultory harangues to which intelligent and devout assemblies are sometimes subjected.

But to sum up all in one word, the minister might have an exemplified Directory or Liturgy of his own, such as was common in all the early and some of the modern Presbyterian churches. If the only objection would be, the labor of composing or compiling it, we hope yet to show that this is an objection which can easily be avoided.

CHAPTER V.

CONGREGATIONAL NEGLECTS, AND THEIR REMEDIES UNDER THE DIRECTORY.

WHATEVER may be the abuses and evils in the ministerial department of our public worship, we believe them to be fully equalled by those which prevail in that of the congregation; and because the latter are the parties primarily interested, their peculiar errors, as well as rights and duties, should be all the more freely canvassed. It would, indeed, be much pleasanter to picture our whole theory, realized both in a ministry endowed with apostolic gifts, and in assemblies rapt in pentecostal fervors; but let it be remembered that the very first step towards amendment, is to deal honestly with the facts as we find them.

And we, therefore, affirm it to be as undeniable as it is lamentable, that in many of our congregations a growing suppression has been taking the place of all proper expression of devotional feeling. Judging by appearances, in some cases, the great mass would seem no longer to go to church to worship God, so much as to hear choirs and sermons. They sit between the pulpit and the organ, in mute compliance, while their prayers and praises are performed by proxy. With all our boasted Protestantism, we have in the heart of our communion the essence of the Roman ritual, a *vicarious service*, of which the people are but auditors, and in which, sometimes, they can no more individually participate than if priest and choir were praying and singing for them in a separate performance.

Some signal exceptions, indeed, there may be to this general decline of congregational worship; but the mournful fact is conspicuous, that our assemblies, as a class, neither "praise God in a becoming manner, with their voices, as well as with their hearts," nor intelligently unite in "offering up their desires to God for things agreeable to his will." Those solemn functions have been delegated to the choir and the preacher, in whose hands they have become respectively mere artistic performances, and individual rhapsodies. In many cases the people do not, simply because they cannot, pray or sing; and the words, "Let us pray." or "Let us sing," are but dead formulas—hints of a duty, echoes of a reality.

It is sometimes urged, in extenuation of these abuses, that the several parts of divine service ought to be thus committed to qualified proxies, in order that by the free exercise of their superior gifts, under the influence of the Holy Ghost, the body of worshippers shall be edified; and the example of the primitive Christian assemblies is cited as an illustration. We need not deny the general doctrine, while we insist that it should at least be carefully and consistently applied. That is unquestionably the most edifying form of public worship, in which those most gifted in prayer and praise shall lead, while the rest of the assembly accompany or follow them; but even the inspired prophets and many-tongued psalmists, in the early Church, were admonished by the apostle to be intelligible, as well as fervent, and on no pretence to intrude mere private rhapsody into public worship. And how much less excusable is any such abuse or misuse of gifts in a modern assembly? If it be granted that the minister or the chorister "edifieth himself," can it be said that "the church is edified"? And when it is plain that neither party is edified; that the public praises are a mere display of musical art, and the public prayers a mere exposure of personal feelings, and even conceits, prejudices, and errors, "how shall he that occupieth the room of the unlearned (laymen or private person) say Amen?" We sometimes hear the devotions criticised not less freely than the sermon as "interesting," "impressive," "beautiful," "eloquent," or the reverse of these. Is it conceivable that this was what the Apostle meant by "excelling in spiritual gifts, to the edifying of the Church," or can such performances themselves, in any proper sense, be regarded as "social acts of homage to the Most High God"?

And the natural effect of this vicarious system has been, not only to rob the people of their prayers and praises, but to destroy all wholesome relish on their part for more congregational worship, if not, in some cases, to foster a depraved taste for the *impressive*, rather than the *expressive* forms of religious service. How could this be otherwise? The worshipper, from being a passive auditor, easily becomes a mere critic of the whole performance, and craves only what shall pleasantly affect his ear or his imagination, or readily fall in with his taste and prejudices. According as the choir do their part, well or ill, he approves or disapproves. If his devotional feeling is sometimes stirred by the preacher, it is at other times hindered. And thus he becomes more regardful of the human agents in worship, than of the Divine majesty and presence, and loses that sense of individual responsibility, which would be sustained and kept awake, were he expressing his own feeling by actually taking part, audibly and intelligently, with others in common acts of devotion.

Now, it must be admitted that these are, to some extent, necessary evils, not absolutely peculiar to our system of worship; and that the most direct and effective remedy for them is to be sought in the cultivation of an earnest and spiritual piety, on the part of both ministers and people. It is, indeed, most true, that did both parties habitually live near to God, and come together in the church full of the Holy Ghost, our worshipping assemblies would be shaken as with a mighty wind of holy fervor, and pray and sing as with tongues of flame; and in times of revival, we are brought to some faint appreciation of this lost ideal. But it is sheer folly, in the face of such facts as have been detailed, to act upon a theory fit only for prophets and psalmists, and even by them only too soon and sadly perverted; and if we would escape that spasmodic type of piety, which at once necessitates and abuses revivals of religion, we must not, in ordinary times at least, disdain the means of normal, healthy growth and culture.

We would, therefore, advocate the use of any right expedients which can be devised for bringing the congregation into more direct sympathy and outward union with the minister, and with one another, in their common devotions. Nothing which can further such important ends is too insignificant to be considered. In social services, such a trifle as gathering together a thin, scattered assembly, into a compact body, will free them from the sense of formality and coldness that would otherwise prevail; and in more public services, a similar benefit might be attained by bringing the minister down from his stilted pulpit, and the choir out of their distant loft, and more visibly and audibly associating them with the mass of their fellow-worshippers. But without dwelling upon such details, we will limit ourselves to one or two general suggestions, which we believe to be legitimate and practical.

1. It would greatly promote congregational devotion, or true public worship, to restore to the whole assembly their peculiar privilege and bounden duty of "praising God by singing psalms or hymns, publicly in the church."* There is that in the very act of such vocal utterance which is fitted to express and nourish holy feeling; and choirs, organs, choristers, or precentors, only succeed in their vocation in so far as they develope it from the mass of worshippers. It is accordingly recommended in the Directory, "that we cultivate some knowledge of the rules of music," and that "the whole congregation should be furnished with books, and ought to join in this part of worship;" for both of which duties excellent provision has been made in our Psalmodist and Hymn Book. It may be questioned, however, whether either Rouse's or Watts's version of the Psalms is to be preferred, either on the score of poetry, or of music, or of devotion, to the literal version chanted by the choir and people. The responsive reading of the Psalter, though only confusing, and anything but solemn to one not taking part in it, has, however, the recommendation that it engages the attention, and helps the devotion of every worshipper; since all may read, though all cannot sing.

2. It would also be a great improvement, if the congregation could join more intelligently in the public prayers, as well as praises, by being no less positively

---

* Directory, Chap. iv.

associated with the minister than with the chorister. We cannot see any such intrinsic difference between the two services as to demand the diverse practice respecting them. If it is indispensable, in the nature of the case, to extemporize the prayers, why not also to improvise the hymns? or if an assembly may devoutly use forms of praise, may they not as devoutly use forms of prayer? The mere intellectual effort of composing or following extemporaneous productions, in the solemn act of public devotion, is very often unfavorable to simple, earnest feeling. The listener becomes entangled with the speaker in sentence-making, or is repelled by expressions or sentiments which, to say the least, he cannot readily adopt and offer up as his own. But, could both parties agree, as touching what things they will ask, and unite together in the use of the same words, there would certainly be less to hinder or distract their common act of worship.

Whether audible responses ought also to be added, as a further help to congregational devotion, is a question of usage and taste, rather than of principle. It cannot be denied, that in the ancient Jewish and early Christian assemblies, the "private person," as the phrase, "he that occupieth the room of the unlearned" might be properly rendered, was wont literally to "say Amen." And when we hear the fervid ejaculations of the Methodists on the one side, and the methodical responses of Episcopalians on the other, we cannot affirm the custom to be in itself either undevout or indecorous. Nor can it be proved to be wholly un-presbyterian. In our early liturgies, says the author of "Eutaxia," "the prayers, by constant use made familiar to the people, were to be followed silently, or in subdued tones." The minister invited the people to make the Confession of Sins, "following in heart these words," or "sincerely saying." And perhaps this mental accompaniment and silent Amen are to be preferred, on the whole, either to the noisy outcries or the confused murmuring of our neighbors. The main thing is, that the attention and devotion be easily sustained, and whether the voice join or respond, is immaterial, if only the minister's form, (for some form every minister does and must have,) be so *simple, suitable,* and *well-known,* that each worshipper can follow it without intellectual fatigue or confusion, and with a fully assenting mind.

Besides the *Amen* in ancient worship was used the *Selah,* or pause for silent devotion, which though also designed as a "rest" in the musical performance of praise, might equally well, in accordance with modern usage, be employed for prayer. As there are times or moods in which the minister will be prompted to fresh, unpremeditated utterances, for which no formulary can make due provision, so there may be occasions, in solemn assemblies, especially in time of communion at the Lord's table, when intervals of silence will conduce far more than speech to true spiritual worship. Let us not disdain devotional helps, from whatever source they may be taken, but remember that no usage becomes widely prevalent which is not founded in some legitimate want of human nature, whether it be the speechless Quaker meeting, or the revival Exhortation, or the random Amen and Hallelujah of the Methodist, or the formal Litany and Collects of the Episcopalian. It is rather the dictate of wisdom to cull out the good from the evil, and, if possible, avoid the abuses and extremes of a partial system, by combining occasional free prayer of the minister, and silent prayer of the worshiper, with stated prayers for the whole congregation.

3. It would complete the ideal we are framing, if the congregation, besides thus participating both in the prayers and in the praises, could also intelligently follow the minister through his scheme of lessons, psalms, and hymns, for each Sunday of the yearly course, by means of a service-book or manual, companion to our Directory and Hymn-book. Whatever might be the advantage to the pastor of such a scheme, that to the people would be ten-fold greater, as it would bring them into perfect sympathy with him, and render their public worship what it ought to be—a systematic instruction in the whole letter of Scripture, together with an intelligent offering up unto God of those ordinary prayers and praises which are proper to every Christian assembly.

In a word, supposing such a system of divine service to have been composed or compiled, in any case where the parties should be mutually so disposed, the minister and congregation might agree, under the general rules of our Directory, (as, indeed, has already been done in at least one instance,*) to conduct their public devotions by the aid of a liturgy. There are, we are aware, grave prejudices and objections to this, which ought to be duly weighed; and we therefore propose to consider them in another chapter.

CHAPTER VI.

THE CONSISTENCY OF A FREE LITURGY WITH THE DIRECTORY.

"THE Directory for Public Worship," as the name itself implies, is a manual of directions for the regulation of ministers and congregations in performing divine service, and differs from a Liturgy in being a prescription of thoughts rather than of words, of rules rather than of materials of devotion; it being left to the discretion of the parties whether such materials shall be extemporized or formulated. The use of a Prayer-book in connection with it would, it is plain, be no more inconsistent with its theory or structure than is the use of a Hymn-book, provided the prayers, as the hymns, were orthodox and suitable; and such a combination, we know, actually prevailed at one time in the Church of England.†

---

* See the "Church Book of St. Peter's Church." Rochester. N. Y.

† While Presbytery was established it was made a penal offence to use the *Prayer-book*, as while Episcopacy was established it was made a penal offence to hold a *Prayer-meeting*; but there were then, as there are now, some, both Episcopalians and Presbyterians, who took the liberty to have either, according to circumstances. Compare Lightfoot's Journal of the Assembly of Divines: Complete Works, vol. xiii. p. 323, 341. and Lathbury's History of the Prayer Book, p. 290; Hall's Lit. Reliq., vol. i. p. 38.

We are met, however, on the threshold of the question, by a prejudice and a misconception, neither of which we believe to be reasonable or truly Presbyterian.

Of the prejudice, which does undoubtedly prevail, let it be said, in the first place, that it is by no means universal, but has taken root most widely and deeply in the Scotch and Scotch-Irish portions of our Church. We do not wish to be misunderstood. It is one of the chief excellencies of our system, whereby its true catholicity is approved, that it is of no mere national or local origin, and cannot be absorbed in any single ecclesiastical organization, such as the Church of Rome, or the Church of England, or the Church of Scotland; but flourishes in all lands, in connection with all races, and under all political systems. Besides the Scotch type of Presbytery, we have the Dutch, the German, the French, and the English; and these several elements have been so fused together in our American communion, and in almost every Presbyterian family that has been long enough in the country, that no true son of such a Church can be suspected of blaming or praising one to the disparagement or advantage of the other. While, therefore, we hold to the staunch orthodoxy of John Knox in opposing all relics of Papal superstition and error in the public worship of God, we may, now at least, demur to his destructive zeal against a certain Book of Common Prayers, about which his conscience was straitened in the time of the Frankfort persecutions,* but concerning which, even then, he could draw from his teacher, John Calvin,† no harsher sentence than that it contained *multas tolerabiles ineptias* (many endurable trifles); and if our subsequent history

---

* Knox, however, was not opposed to the contents of the Prayer-book *in toto*, but rather to its accompanying ceremonies. He could, and did, use it when in England, omitting, by permission of Cranmer, the parts he disliked; and his reason for not accepting a benefice in London was, that he was "not willing to be *bound* to use King Edward's book *entire*." See "The Puritans and Queen Elizabeth," by Samuel Hopkins, pp. 77, 78, vol. i.

† After Knox had returned to Scotland, Calvin again writes to him in 1561: "With regard to ceremonies, I trust, even should you displease many, that you will moderate your rigor." Calvin's Letters. Trans. by Jules Bonnet. Vol. iv. p. 184.

as to other church questions be all that we could desire, yet we may begin to query whether we have succeeded as well in adjusting the liturgical problem; and whether, upon the whole, such learned and godly Presbyterians as Thomas Manton, Edmund Calamy, William Bates, Richard Baxter, did not show better logic and wisdom in striving to purge out the *tolerabiles ineptias*, than to throw away the gold with the dross. The truth is, that throughout all these troubles, our Church was passing between the two fires of Prelacy and Independency, liturgy and conventicle — escaping unhurt, indeed, though not without marks of the flame; and to this day the motto of the mother Kirk still suits the dilemma of her American daughter—*Nec tamen consumebatur*, with the difference, that we now lean too near to the Puritan, to be in any danger of the Ritualist.

But, in the second place, it could easily be shown that even our Scotch prejudice against liturgies is both unintelligent and inconsistent. The simple fact is, that the Church of Scotland, although at present non-liturgical, is not, and never has been anti-liturgical, but was driven into its negative position by "the unjustifiable efforts of Laud and his master to force a justly obnoxious liturgy upon a free people;"* and as one of the ill effects of that unhappy controversy, we inherit a morbid terror of everything approaching to form in public worship. But the earlier usage, even in the days of Knox, as we have seen, was very different. "The Book of Common Order, or the Order of the English Kirk at Geneva, whereof John Knox was Minister: approved by the famous and learned man, John Calvin; received and used by the Reformed Kirk of Scotland, and ordinarily prefixed to the Psalms in Metre: A. D. 1600," has all the elements of a complete liturgy, and contains, in common with the Prayer-book, as parts of the ordinary service, a Confession of Sins, the Lord's Prayer, the Apostles' Creed, a Prayer for the whole estate of Christ's Church, &c., besides the marriage service nearly verbatim, the ceremony of the

---

* Eutaxia, p. 250.

ring excepted. We have seen under what pressure of Prelacy on the one side, and dragging of Independency on the other, we were at length forced away from both these liturgies into the Directory. But it is surely neither wise nor consistent to continue under the dominion of a prejudice due to such causes.

There is, however, in connection with this prejudice, a misconception which has, no doubt, tended to strengthen and perpetuate it, and which may even remain after it has been exposed, or where it does not prevail. We refer to the common mistake of confounding a liturgy with an artistic ritual or elaborate ceremonial service. The very word is associated in some minds with those objects of Puritan dislike, the altar, the surplice, the sign of the cross, bowing in the creed, and all the paraphernalia of a scenic worship. What has been described, however, in these pages, has nothing to do with such accessories, and would be imperilled by admixture with them.* We have advocated no particular style of church architecture and furniture, or of ministerial dress, or of congregational behavior, and have proposed no innovations in such matters; but, leaving them where the Directory leaves them, have simply maintained that there might be, and, in some cases, there ought to be, in connection with the

---

* It was from no dislike of art, in itself and in its own sphere, but only from an anxiety to guard the more vital interests of religion, that the Calvinistic cultus, in distinction from the Lutheran, became so strongly impressed with an aspect of sobriety and simplicity. "We must not forget," says a learned critic of both systems, "that it was people of the South, among whom Calvin as a Reformer specially labored. Ceremonies which, in a nation with the more earnest and tranquil character of the Germans, Luther could retain, without a thought of their being abused, not without ground appeared dubious in the case of the most excitable Southern temperament, which only too soon would have clung to that which is outward; and since Calvin well knew that Catholicism, with all its gorgeous splendor, and its superstitions resting on dim pretensions and emotions, was the offspring of the glowing South, he must, even on this ground, have found it necessary, in order to preserve the evangelical doctrine from all commingling with Catholicism, to present it outwardly also in rugged antithesis to that system." The Sunday Service according to the Liturgies of the Churches of the Reformation, by Rev. C. P. Krauth, D. D., Editor of the Lutheran and Missionary.

faithful preaching of God's word, a system of common devotions for both minister and people, whereby they could methodically become acquainted with the Holy Scriptures, and statedly, by simple spiritual acts of worship, offer up their public prayers and praises "with the spirit and with the understanding also." With the Presbyterian divines at the Savoy Conference, we have judged that "Prayer, confession, thanksgiving, reading of the Scriptures, and administration of the sacraments, in the plainest and simplest manner, were matter enough to furnish out a sufficient liturgy, though nothing either of private opinion, or of church pomp, of garments, or prescribed gestures, of imagery, of music, of matter concerning the dead, of many superfluities which creep into the Church under the name of *order* and *decency*, did interpose itself."[*]

Such a liturgy we believe to be not only consistent with true Presbyterianism, but a legitimate development of it, which has hitherto been hindered by untoward influences, and which is already urgently needed to defend the weak point of our system, and equip it for the work of church extension in all directions. And its judicious introduction by agreement of the two parties concerned, need not occasion any interference with the rights of those congregations which prefer a different usage, nor any more serious diversity than already, and of necessity, prevails in our practice.

Of the objections that may be raised to such a liturgy, the most plausible is, that it would tend to formalism in worship. We do not wish to slur this objection, but to sift it as thoroughly as can be, in the absence of a fair experiment, by which alone the question could be decided. It would indeed be but right to first take into account the alternative evils to which we are exposed. There may be such things as hypocrisy, cant, extravagance, and superstition, as well as formality in divine service; and when there is no fresh impulse or occasion of devotion, it will not be strange, it will simply be unavoidable, that, in the absence of a

---

[*] The Exceptions against the Book of Common Prayer. Document XV.

well-ordered form to excite and cherish holy feeling, there should be forced or feigned excitement. We are not speaking of what ought to be, but of what are, the facts. Let us not deceive ourselves, but look at the question on all sides, and we may possibly reach the conclusion, that at times a liturgy might prove a help rather than a hinderance to true spiritual worship. When the minister's spirit is clouded and heavy, his written sermon is a great relief, and may even gradually warm him up into genuine fervor, and his whole audience with him; or if he eschew preparation and paper, and halt and trip in his utterance, large excuses can still be made for one who comes speaking to the people in the name of God; but when he turns to speak to God in the name of the people, is it perfectly reasonable that the devotions of some hundreds of worshippers should be left dependent upon his bodily condition? The spirit may be willing, but the flesh is weak. He might, perhaps, take some old familiar words in company with them, and at least not hinder their devotion or his own; but to absolutely make new prayers for them, *ex tempore*, every Sunday, under dread of falling into a *form* of prayer—alas! is it not enough that he should make two able and eloquent sermons?

Some form there must be, in all edifying worship. Without it, we relapse towards Methodist extravagance or Quaker apathy. Some form there is in every pastor's mode of conducting worship. He glides into a service almost as stereotyped as the dreaded liturgy. It is, after all, the thing without the name; and the only question really worth considering, is, whether that liturgy shall be a good one or a bad one. The advocates of a supposed impromptu service, springing up in perennial freshness, and ceaseless variety, do not seem rightly to distinguish between public and private devotion, or between ordinary and extraordinary states of religious feeling. In social meetings, especially during seasons of revival, or on marked providential occasions, the whole outward expression of worship will indeed be free and artless, and any thing like forms would be felt as an intolerable bondage; but in large assemblies, convened for stated acts of homage, there cannot but be more of system, sameness, and pre-arrangement. Nor is it easy to see what advantage would be gained by an ingenious variety, or capricious novelty, so far as that is possible in reference to the ordinary devotions of a congregation, when there might be customary forms of expressing them, which have been used and sanctioned by the learned and godly of all churches and ages; which being largely taken from the very words of Scripture, concisely express the wants, the fears, the doubts, the hopes, and the joys of all Christians; and which are marked by a simple majesty of style, a chaste fervor, tenderness, and solemnity, utterly unknown in any modern compositions. In the open, voluntary use of such helps to devotion, both parties might find a mutual relief and profit, which must be foregone so long as either the people are at the mercy of random effusions, or the minister is hampered with a surreptitious form of his own.

We may add, that the objection now under consideration is not supported by facts. Some of the most spiritually-minded men that ever lived, have used and contended for a liturgy; but formalists will be formal under any system.

Another and kindred objection is, that a liturgy would repress all originality on the part of the minister, and foster a deadly monotony in his services. The life of public worship, it is argued, consists in that vivid impression made by an earnest speaker, with heart aglow, and voice and tone spontaneously giving forth every petition as an expression of his own personal feeling. Such prayers, it is said, are more "interesting," "solemn," or "touching," than any recited form, however appropriate. We admit this personal or individual element to be a great advantage in the sermon, and even, with proper limitations, in the service. The very best preaching and praying are confessedly extemporaneous, and also the *very worst*. It depends entirely upon the person, the mood, the occasion, and the circumstances; and when all of these are not perfectly favorable, then the question presents another aspect. The Apostle's rule is, "Let all things be done to edifying;" and there may be, as we have seen, individual peculiarities or originalities in public prayer which are not edifying. Because the broken, confused utterances of some private suppliant are far better for him than any form, it does not follow that they will also be more edifying to a whole assembly, nor is it quite clear that any sentimental advantage or pathetic interest gained by their exposure, is not more than balanced by the risk of a certain vanity, embarrassment, or indelicacy, on the one side, together with a certain admiration, regret, or pity, on the other. Ah! it may be pardonable in us to like to hear a good sermon; but is it worshipping God to like to hear how well a *man* can pray? and do we not sometimes see the "gift of prayer" without the grace, as well as the grace without the gift?

Moreover, the objection we are considering is valid only on the assumption, that the minister is so slavishly tied down to rules and forms, that he cannot, when the fresh mood or new occasion prompts him, break away from them into more spontaneous services. It would, of course, be impossible to frame either directions or samples for every possible emergency; and the only proper design of a liturgy is, to give edifying expression to those stated public devotions, which are in their nature fixed and invariable, while all the benefits of the most informal worship may still be sufficiently retained in the lecture and prayer-meetings during the week, or in the second service on the Lord's day, as well as by blending free with stated prayer, on all occasions, at discretion.

A far more specious scruple is, that liturgies foster an "æsthetical" form of devotion, or cultivate the taste and imagination at the expense of the heart and conscience. Some persons, it is asserted, are of a liturgical temperament, and by dwelling critically upon the form in distinction from the matter or spirit of worship, at length become so fastidious, that they are in danger of making their whole religion little better than one of the fine arts; and this, it is maintained, is a weakness and folly, which ought to be mortified rather than humored.

It need not be denied that there may be an excess of even so good a thing as good taste; but, on the other hand, it must be confessed that the holiest things may be spoiled by so trifling a thing as a little bad taste. And when Presbyterian congregations, on all sides, are to be found worshipping in imitation Parthenons and Westminsters, with the aid of costly music and oratory, we may fairly question, what should be the literary character of their liturgy; and, whether it would not be wiser, safer, and more consistent to give vent to the irrepressible æsthetic element in the form of a reasonable service, than to lavish it upon artistic surroundings, so little in keeping with the traditional simplicity of our worship.

It is also sometimes objected that forms of devotion, and especially those in the Prayer-book, are suited only to the worldly classes of society, and to such as are content with a superficial type of Christianity. Even Episcopalian dissent, we are told, with the prestige of a court ritual, is undermining "the Church" in Scotland; the whole fashionable class in our own country are assuming a liturgical mode of worship as one of their prerogatives; and its general adoption in the present state of things, could only relax the terms of communion, and obscure or weaken the vital distinction between the Church and the world.

We have no disposition to make light of such apprehensions. Let it be freely granted, as experience both in the Old and the New world has shown, that an *imposed* liturgy does thus cramp the evangelizing power of the ministry, and foster caste, fashion, and worldliness; yet this could not be charged against an *optional* liturgy to be used or forborne, according to the varying exigency of places and occasions. Nor should we disguise it from ourselves that, without some flexible agency of this kind, we are in danger of losing our hold upon those educated classes who really form the brain and virtue of the state. It is in fact the mission of a true Church of Christ to embrace within itself both extremes of the social scale, and so mould and re-adjust all ranks and conditions, as to render them but various members of one and the same mystical body.

As to the objection, that it would cost us something of church pride and consistency, or expose us to ridicule as imitators, if this be so, it is enough to say, in view of the historical facts already presented, that the sooner all parties are rid of such ideas the better.

The only remaining difficulty we now think of is, the want of a suitable manual or service-book, sanctioned by sufficient Presbyterian authority to insure its orthodoxy, and encourage its use. We believe this objection to be the most serious that can be raised; but by no means insuperable, as we hope may appear in our next chapter.

CHAPTER VII.

THE WARRANT FOR THE PRESBYTERIAN VERSION OF THE PRAYER-BOOK.

In our previous essays we have advocated these three means of correcting and improving our public worship: 1st. In all cases a careful attention to the rules and suggestions of the Directory ; 2d. In many cases a system of services, with forms or examples, composed or compiled by the minister for his own assistance ; 3d. In some cases, where the parties are so agreed, a liturgy, or scheme of common devotions, for both minister and congregation, containing not merely psalms and hymns, and Directory, but tables of Scripture lessons, forms of stated prayer, and of administration of the sacraments, and other rites of the Church. Advancing a step farther, we desire now to show that either or all of these advantages can be secured in an edition of the Book of Common Prayer, as revised by the Royal Commission of Presbyterian Divines, at the Savoy Conference, A. D. 1661, and in agreement with our Directory for Public Worship.

As this was with the writer no foregone conclusion, but a wholly unforeseen result of some studies and efforts in the direction of a truly Presbyterian liturgy, he begs the reader, who has followed him thus far, to candidly review the several historical facts upon which it is based, and the arguments upholding it.

1. *The Prayer-book was set aside for the Directory by the Westminster divines on avowed principles which admit of its resumption.* In their Preface, after recounting the evils then arising out of its forcible imposition upon the churches, they thus declared their motives:

"Upon these, and many the like weighty considerations, in reference to the whole Book in general, and because of divers particulars contained in it: not from any love to novelty, or intention to disparage our first reformers, (of whom we are persuaded that were they now alive, they would join with us in this work, and whom we acknowledge as excellent instruments, raised by God, to begin the purging and building of his house, and desire they may be had of us and posterity in everlasting remembrance, with thankfulness and honor.) but that we may, in some measure, answer the gracious providence of God, which at this time calleth upon us for further reformation, and may satisfy our own consciences, and answer the expectation of other reformed churches, and the desires of many of the godly among ourselves, and withal give some public testimony of our endeavors for uniformity in Divine worship, which we have promised in our 'Solemn League and Covenant.' We have, after earnest and frequent calling upon the name of God, and after much consultation, not with flesh and blood, but with his holy word, resolved to lay aside the former liturgy, with the many rites and ceremonies, formerly used in the worship of God, and have agreed upon this following Directory for all the parts of public worship, at ordinary and extraordinary times."

We believe that both the spirit and the letter of these cautious declarations favor the point we are arguing. When it is remembered that the Directory was mainly a semi-political device,* resulting from the opposite forces of prelacy and independency, and that it utterly failed to secure the "covenanted uniformity," for which it was originally framed; and when it is remembered that the objections therein enumerated against the Prayer-book, such as the imposition of things indifferent as

---

* The Parliamentary order to the Assembly of Divines was, that they should confer and treat among themselves "concerning the Directory of Worship, *or liturgy hereafter* to be in the Church." The subject occupied them more than two months, and the result was a compromise of the Scotch Commissioners with the Independents, and of both with the English Presbyterians. To escape discussion a very disproportionate number of the former, were appointed on the Committee to prepare the Preface. See Hetherington's History of Westminster Assembly, pp. 153, 154. Lightfoot's Journal of Westminster Assembly, Vol. xiii. p. 17. Baird's Book of Public Prayer, Intro. p. xv.

terms of communion, the suppression of free prayer and preaching, the obtrusion of new papistical ceremonies, and the maintenance of an unedifying, beneficed clergy, were chargeable to the mere political and sectarian surroundings of the book, rather than to its contents, duly purged and amended; and when, moreover, it is remembered that we, in this land and age of greater light and freedom, are no longer harassed by the untoward influences, and driven to the rash extremes, which this liturgy then occasioned, and that all former difficulties in regard to its use, in our present necessities and opportunities, have subsided into mere inherited prejudices; we shall surely not be inconsistent, to say the least, if we return to it as to the work of our revered forefathers, and thereby again illustrate our dearly bought liberty, as well to resume and modify it, as to lay it aside according to the varying exigency of times and occasions. And, lest it be thought we misrepresent them, let the simple fact which afterwards followed be next considered.

2. *The Prayer-book was actually revised by the framers of the Directory, and their associates, with a view to its resumption.* Among the Presbyterian Commissioners at the Savoy Conference, were some of the most distinguished Westminster divines;* and their own immortal writings still rank as the authorized standards of our church.† Both as scholars and theologians they

---

*Tuckney, Calamy, Spurstow, Wallis, Case, Reynolds, Newcomen, Conant, Lightfoot, etc.

† Tuckney and Reynolds were members of the Committee which framed our Confession of Faith. Tuckney, Arrowsmith, and Newcomen were the committee to prepare the Larger Catechism, the principal part of which was in the very words of Tuckney. Thus the name first among the revisers of the Prayer-book, had also been first among the framers of our standards. See History of the Westminster Assembly, compiled for the Board of Publication, from the best authorities, pp. 348, 383. The composition of the Shorter Catechism is commonly attributed to Wallis, see Hetherington's History of the Westminster Assembly, p. 261. Reid's Memoirs of the Lives and writings of the Westminster Divines, p 187.

See the "Non-Conformist's Memorial"; being an account of the Lives, Sufferings and Printed Works, of the two thousand Ministers ejected from the Church of England.

were unequalled,* either then or since, and were not despised even by their adversaries, who proffered them the highest honors of that Church establishment which, with the spirit of martyrs, they afterwards abandoned. It cannot be charged, much less proved upon such men, that they were of a compliant or compromising temper. While, as they declared, they had "not the least thought of depraving or reproaching the Book of Common Prayer," yet their "exceptions" against it were not only "general," but "particular" or verbal, with a degree of scrupulous minuteness that would now be deemed superfluous; and these "exceptions," having never been fairly acted upon by both parties, have come down to us without a trace or taint of concession. We have, in fact, all the materials of a thoroughly Presbyterian edition of the Prayer-book in the form of such historical documents as the following:

1. "The King's Warrant for the Conference at the Savoy."
2. "The Exceptions of the Presbyterian Ministers against the Book of Common Prayer," (including a written criticism upon both text and rubric, with proposed alterations, emendations, and additions.)
3. "The Answer of the Bishops to the Exceptions of the Ministers."
4. "The Petition for Peace and Concord, presented to the Bishops, with the proposed Reformation of the Liturgy."
5. "The Rejoinder of the Ministers to the Answer of the Bishops—the Grand Debate between the most Reverend the Bishops and the Presbyterian Divines, appointed by his sacred Majesty, as Commissioners for the Review and Alteration of the Book of Common Prayer, &c., being an exact account of their whole proceedings. The most perfect copy. London, 1661: pp. 1—148."†

---

*See "An Account of the Ministers, Lecturers, Masters and Fellows of Colleges who were silenced or ejected by the Act of Uniformity in 1661. Designed for the preserving to Posterity, the Memory of their Names, Characters, Writings, and Sufferings," in two vols., by Edmund Calamy, D. D. London, 1713. Also the same enlarged, and edited by Palmer, in 3 vols., entitled the "Non-Conformist's Memorial, being an account of the Lives, Sufferings, and Printed Works, of the two thousand Ministers ejected from the Church of England."

† As collateral aids may also be used, the present English Prayer-book with its Presbyterian emendations, for which the most reverend Bishops in their Preface (see the English edition) thought fit to apologize; the proposed Prayer-book of 1689, which was framed in consultation with the leaders of the ejected Presbyterians, and which, in the opinion of Calamy, would have satisfied more than

The Book, as revised and amended by the aid of these documents, could not be chargeable with any private or modern fancies, but would embody the matured suggestions of learned and godly men, who were lawfully charged with the work of revision, and who, in that good work, endured great temptation and persecution. And the whole, besides being a worthy memorial of our Church forefathers, would be at least as truly Presbyterian as our present service-book, which contains a Directory of Worship, originally framed by ordained ministers of the Church of England, "with the assistance of Commissioners from the Church of Scotland," * and a collection of hymns compiled from all accessible sources. But the last shred of an objection, on the score of consistent Presbyterianism, must disappear before our next consideration.

3. As the Directory is but a skeleton of the Prayer-book, so the *Prayer-book itself is but a compilation which is more Presbyterian than Episcopalian in its sources.* We mean simply to say that, leaving out of view those portions which belong exclusively to neither party, but have been sanctioned and used by both, (being derived from ancient Christian liturgies, and from Lutheran formularies,) the remainder, which is by no means inconsiderable in character or quantity, is almost entirely Presbyterian. This is unquestionably true of the Book as revised by the Savoy Presbyterians, and it is sufficiently true for this argument, of the Book as it is now familiar to the American reader; as will appear from the following general reference to its historical sources.†

The Exhortation, General Confession, Declaration of Absolution, and General Thanksgiving, in the Order for Daily Prayer, and the Ten Commandments as they appear in the Ante-Communion Office, are admitted to be

---

two-thirds of their number; and the different Presbyterian editions, dating before the Savoy Conference, especially the Second Book of King Edward VI., to which the Presbyterian Commissioners constantly appealed.

* Of the one hundred and twenty divines in the Westminster Assembly, five were Commissioners from the Church of Scotland, six or seven were Independents, several were Episcopalians, and the remainder were English Presbyterians.

† See Chapter ix. for a more particular analysis.

of Calvinistic origin. All that remains (except the apocryphal Song and Lessons,) viz., the Te Deum, the Litany, the Creeds, the Collects, Epistles, and Gospels, have passed from their ancient sources through Presbyterian sanctions, and under a Presbyterian revision. to their present form. In other words, the whole Lord's day service, as usually performed, contains but a single prayer* that can be traced to a distinctively Episcopalian origin; and for the obvious reason, partly, that that service was framed before the assertion of Prelacy against Presbytery arose. and also that its Protestant additions and emendations are almost exclusively from Calvinistic sources.

In the occasional Offices of Baptism, Matrimony, Visitation of the Sick, and Burial of the Dead, the question of authorship lies between the Calvinist and the Lutheran, or between the French and the German Protestant, rather than between the Presbyterian and the Episcopalian. While portions of those formularies are clearly traceable to the Cologne liturgy of the Calvinistic Bucer and Melanchthon, yet, having thus originated outside of the pretentious Anglican Prelacy, they belong to the general class of Reformed or Protestant *non*-Episcopal rituals, and as such, might have continued in actual use, but for certain doubtful expressions and superstitious ceremonies, by which they were vitiated, and from which our ecclesiastical fathers in the Savoy Conference strove to purge them.

As to the Psalter, it is well known that it was first restored to the people, in the form of congregational psalmody, in the Church of Geneva, from whence it was copied, as a popular element of worship in the English churches.

Of the whole compilation, indeed, except the Ordinal or ordination services, and several political or State services, added after the Savoy Revision, it is safe to affirm, that were it amended according to that revision, it would be as thoroughly Presbyterian in its historical sources sa well as sanctions, and, in fact, in every thing

---

* Even this exception is doubtful. See Chapter lx. "Prayer for all Conditions of Men."

but its present popular associations, as the book now used in our pulpits and pews. The almost universal impression to the contrary has arisen out of the false assumption that our forefathers were as much opposed to Liturgy as Prelacy, or to the literary contents of the Prayer-book, as to the tyrannical statutes and superstitious rites accompanying it. It is forgotten, or no longer known among us, that the Presbyterian Church in England, with her two thousand clergy, her scholars, divines, and patriots of illustrious memory, her prestige of learning, rank, and power, in the act of giving up, for conscience' sake, the high places and rich livings of an establishment which owed its restoration to her loyalty, also abandoned a liturgy to which her ministers had an hereditary right, upon the basis of which their adversaries were legally compelled to meet them in conference for their satisfaction, and which, at the same time, they declared they had "not the least thought of depraving or reproaching." And this hard alternative* into which they were driven by the exigencies of a State religion, in an age of sectarian rancor and violence, we have thoughtlessly accepted and continued as our sole, normal condition. But surely, after two centuries of peaceful progress, in another country, under a government of equal laws, and in the midst of spontaneous tendencies towards a free, spiritual liturgy, it is high time to ask if there be not some safe mean between the wild extremes from which we have so happily escaped, and whether

---

* The question has been asked, why the Presbyterian clergy did not set up their revised Liturgy or reformed Prayer-book, outside of the Established Church? But it must be remembered that like the Scotch Presbyterians, they contended for the principle of an Establishment, and but a short time before, by Acts of King and Parliament, legally formed part of it; and moreover, it was only through political intrigue that they lost their former control of it; the "Act of Uniformity," in plain violation of the Royal Declaration, having been expressly so framed as to drive them beyond its pale, strip them of their orders, and place them under civil disabilities which were only removed by the "Act of Toleration" in 1698, when an effort was made, by a new Commission, for their "Comprehension" in the Establishment; but owing to various causes, "this great and good work at that time miscarried." See Archbishop Tillotson's Works, p. 5, 12. London ed. 1752, and Calamy's Abridgment of Baxter's Hist. of his Life and Times, p. 317.

history has not reserved it as a just providential compensation, that we should now enter into the labors, while we vindicate the fame, of those faithful men "of whom the world was not worthy."

4. Our last and conclusive argument is, that the Prayer-book, thus revised, with our American Directory in place of the English Rubric, *is the only Presbyterian liturgy that is either desirable or practicable.* After what we have stated as to the origin and history of that compilation, we shall not now be suspected of any disloyalty in affirming that, with all its faults, it is simply incomparable. No one who studies the subject, historically and philosophically, can fail to see that it meets the needs of ordinary divine service better than any other formulary that has ever been devised, or become widely prevalent. A fresh worker in this field, taking as his ideal of Christian worship a scheme of stated forms, which should express, in simple Scripture phrase, the common needs of a church assembly, and be redolent of the communion of saints in all lands and ages—such a worker, after all the thought and research he can bestow upon the question, at length finds that he has been anticipated by a book which is framed to fit the mould of the universal Christian heart, which is wrought out of the warp and woof of ancient and modern piety, which contains the cream of all liturgies, both of our own and of other churches, and which has lingering about it a savor of pure and fervent devotion belonging to no other uninspired composition. If he loves our English Bible, he must also love that English liturgy which was the product of the same age, and in the same sacred style. To attempt now any better devotional phraseology would be as vain as to frame a better version of the Holy Scriptures. To attempt any different compilation would be but to glean in fields already reaped and garnered; and to attempt any ingenious recomposition of its materials, would be but to incur the odium of imitation or invasion, where we ought rather to assert an original right of property and inheritance. It has, in fact, been the chief mistake of our liturgical writers hitherto, that, from a well-meant fear of concession or intrusion, they have so generally striven to ignore a collection which has

been culled from the gathered wisdom and piety of the Church universal, and which, after all that has been said and done against it, has continued, for these several centuries past, the only Christian liturgy deserving the name.*

We know very well, indeed, that as now viewed by Presbyterians, it has many serious blemishes and inconveniences, and even pernicious errors,† the still remaining dross of the furnace through which it has passed; but none of these, it will be found, have escaped the searching revision and thorough expurgation of the Savoy divines, or need encumber it in the hands of those who are not trammelled with inflexible rubrics. As combined with a Directory, allowing to the minister his liberty to remedy, at discretion, the tedious length and multiplicity of its services, and neither requiring nor precluding responses, on the part of the congregation, nor indeed demanding any other behaviour than is already customary in our assemblies, it would, we honestly believe, be the best liturgy that could be desired, or now devised.

We will even go further, and declare our conviction that, as it is the only liturgy fit to be used, so it is the only one that can be used with any thing like Presbyterian consistency. The nature of our system, and the nature of the exigency, combine to shut us up to this alternative. On the one hand the wise, generous spirit of our system will not allow the whole Church to be hampered with any thing more liturgical than a Directory; and, on the other hand, the exigency to be met is such, that it cannot be fully supplied by mere private

---

* We do not except the Presbyterian Liturgies of the continent for the reason that they break more entirely with the "Catholic or Universal Church" of the past, than was deemed necessary by the Savoy Presbyterians; and moreover, being of foreign origin and modern translation, are wanting in that solemn scriptural style, peculiar to the old *English* of our Bibles, and so desirable in order to separate the language of public worship from that of ordinary literature and conversation.

† For example, the Baptismal offices and the Ordinal, which, it is well known, are not, in their most natural sense and effect, entirely acceptable even to all Episcopalians, and still less to the great mass of Christians in other churches.

or voluntary efforts. For any single pastor to compose a liturgy, would be as absurd as to compose a hymn-book; and for him to compile one, exclusive of the Prayer-book, would be as impossible as to compile a new creed or psalter. No man or body of men now living could frame any better, or any other formulary, at all answering to the proper idea of a liturgy, than that which our ecclesiastical forefathers in England have first revised, and then bequeathed to us, invested with the halo of martyrdom; and by adopting it as the fruit of their orthodoxy, learning and piety, while we gain all the advantages of authority, antiquity, catholicity, and perfect fitness, we sacrifice neither our liberty, nor our just pride as Presbyterians.*

---

* To say that Presbyterians would become Episcopalians by thus returning to a liturgy inherited and revised by the framers of our own Church standards, is like saying that Episcopalians are becoming Presbyterians because they have begun to discover that the framers of *their* Church standards held to Apostolical succession, if they held it at all, as *presbyterial* rather than episcopal. A series of learned and able articles have lately appeared in the *Episcopal Recorder* in which the writer conclusively shows:

"1. That in the Ordinal, *as it was arranged by Cranmer, Ridley, and their coadjutors*, there is no difference in the words of ordaining, to distinguish the office of Bishop from that of Presbyter. This distinction was not made till one hundred years later, by the Bishops under Charles II.

"2. There is no evidence, in the form itself, that the Reformers regarded the office as a distinct order, derived from Scripture."

And in view of the facts and authorities which he cites, he pertinently asks:

"Is it not evident that the Reformers, if they believed in any doctrine of ministerial succession, regarded it as belonging to the order of presbyters by divine appointment? . . . If the succession is not in the presbyterate by divine right, why did members hold livings by law in the Church of England, who were ordained by presbyters alone, preaching and administering the sacraments to the members of that church for more than a century? What ground, then, is there in the Ordinal (as arranged by the Reformers,) for this boasted personal, tactual, apostolic episcopal succession, which has led to sacramental error, defection to Popery, spread discord in our communion, repelled our fellow christians, and prevented a union of Protestant Christendom?" He also expresses the "confident hope," on behalf of the Episcopalians generally, that these views will "commend them to the respect and confidence of intelligent Christians in their respective churches." See "THE VIEW OF THE CHURCH AND MINISTRY OF CHRIST, as held by the Protestant Episcopal Church, contained in her standards, and explained according to the published expositions of the compilers and revisers

Nor could its use in common with that highly respectable denomination, which meanwhile has arisen in our own country, and so faithfully preserved and honored

---

of the Book of Common Prayer."—*Episcopal Recorder*, Art. ix., March 1863.

While our neighbors are thus proving themselves to be such good Presbyterians, we are tempted to reciprocate, by reminding them that the first American Presbytery, by any test that may be applied to it, is quite as certainly traceable to "the Apostles' time," through the Church of Scotland, as the first American Episcopate, through the Church of England; and although, like the venerable Bishop White, we are somewhat indifferent concerning this question of an Apostolical pedigree, yet it is because we insist only upon our Apostolical doctrine and discipline. Wherever these marks of the true succession appear, we are happy to honor and sanction them, whether in ministers of the Protestant Episcopal Church, or any of its sister denominations. See Alexander's "Essays on the Primitive Church Offices," p. 177.

We have said that Bishop White was somewhat indifferent as to the Episcopal succession. It does not seem to be generally known or remembered, how narrowly that eminent divine and patriot escaped becoming a Presbyterian. In a learned essay which he published at the time of the Revolution, entitled, "*The Case of the Episcopal Churches in the United States Considered*," will be found the "sketch of a frame of government," which so substantially accords with the Constitution of the Presbyterian Church, one cannot but regret that the course of events did not favour its adoption. It proposed a series of representative bodies, corresponding respectively to the Presbytery, Synod, and General Assembly, (p. 12.) with the difference that the Moderator of each Presbytery was to be a permanent officer, to be invested, however, with no exclusive power of ordination or confirmation, and to be burdened with no duty that should "materially interfere with his employments in the station of a parochial clergyman," (p. 11); and as at that time it was objected that "the very name of Bishop is offensive," he was to be entitled "a President, a Superintendent, or in plain English, and according to the literal translation of the original, an Overseer," (p. 19.) The scheme would, indeed, further comprise "a general approbation of Episcopacy, and a declaration of an intention to procure the succession as soon as conveniently may be." But the author himself declares that "the proposal to constitute a frame of government, the execution of which shall depend on the pleasure of persons unknown, differing from us in language, habits, and perhaps in religious principles, has too ludicrous an appearance to deserve consideration," (p. 17); and in view of the existing rupture with the British government, he urges "an immediate execution of the plan, without waiting for the Episcopal succession," "on the presumption that the worship of God, and the instruction and reformation of the people, are the principal objects of ecclesiastical discipline, and to relinquish them from a scrupulous adherence to episcopacy, is sacrificing the substance to the ceremony," (p. 19.) In support of the plan, then follows an admirable argument from history and Scripture against the divine right of episcopacy, (chap. v.,) with this conclusion

it among us, be other than pleasing to any, in either Church, who "profess and call themselves Christians," or who are ready to rejoice at the many and great things in which Christians can agree, as compared with the few and small things in which they differ.

We conclude this part of our subject with two inferences. The one is, that the liturgical question has already been exhausted, so far as discussion could exhaust it, by a former age. The time for mere argument has gone by. We have here presented, not without some needful exaggeration, it may be, a side which Presbyterians have but seldom viewed. We know very well what strong reasonings can be brought from the opposite side; but we know also that no reasonings that could now be brought from either side would equal those of the disputants who were once so terribly in

---

"Now if the form of church government rest on no other foundation than ancient and apostolic *practice*, it is humbly submitted to consideration, whether Episcopalians will not be thought scarcely deserving the name of Christians, should they, rather than consent to a temporary deviation, abandon every ordinance of positive and divine appointment," (p. 25.) He further suggests that "should the episcopal succession afterwards be obtained, any *supposed* imperfections of the intermediate ordinations might, if it were judged proper, be supplied without acknowledging their nullity, by a *conditional* ordination resembling that of *conditional baptism* in the liturgy," (p. 20.); but beyond this very dubious intimation, there is not a sentence to show that "the succession *supposed necessary* to constitute the Episcopal character," (p. 15,) was considered by him to be in any view essential or fundamental.

Eventually, however, as it is well known, circumstances altered "the case of the Episcopal churches," and developed in them a different theory of ecclesiastical polity. The first General Convention petitioned the English Archbishops that they "would be pleased to confer the Episcopal character," and, on certain terms, the petition was granted by Act of Parliament; Bishop White himself being one of the clergymen who crossed the ocean to receive consecration. If this course indicated a radical change of opinions on his part, the above quotations could only appear perplexing to all parties. Under the circumstances, we incline to the hypothesis that, like Bishop Reynolds of Norwich, he continued at heart as good a Presbyterian after as before his promotion to a diocesan charge; for certainly no one can read his able treatise without feeling what the Bishop himself says of a similar work of Stillingfleet, that "the book seems easier RETRACTED than REFUTED," (p. 25.)

The copy from which we quote bears the imprint of William Claypoole, Philadelphia, 1782, and contains the autograph of the learned author.

earnest, as to add battles to their books, diplomacy to their logic, and martyrdom to their orthodoxy

The other inference is, that the whole question is one of the unsolved problems which the Old World has bequeathed to the New. Although so thoroughly canvassed there, yet it was at length settled only by the strong arm of the law, and in a manner that posterity here refuses to accept as final or satisfactory: The Directory of the Established Church of Scotland, and the Liturgy of the Established Church of England, the several fruits of a sectarian warfare, that would permit neither to live but by exterminating the other, cannot now be viewed, in the light of facts around us, as other than rash extremes, from which the free churches of this land are already verging towards a substantial unity, in the midst of trivial diversity.

On the 24th of August last, in the city of London, but out of the Church of England, was commemorated the bi-centenary of that black day in her saints' calendar, the second St. Bartholomew tragedy, which gave her the Prayer-book, without the pledged alterations, at a cost of so many martyrs for Presbyterian orthodoxy and spirituality. Should the same work as here issued on the basis of their revision, and in their name, do aught towards that spiritual "Act of Uniformity," which neither covenants nor statutes could then compel, or now retard, their testimony will not have been in vain.

CHAPTER VIII.

THE HISTORICAL MATERIALS FOR THE PRESBYTERIAN PRAYER-BOOK.

WE have maintained that the problem of a Presbyterian liturgy can only be met and solved by bringing the American Presbyterianism of the Nineteenth Century into contact with the English Presbyterianism of the

Seventeenth Century, through an edition of the Prayer-book, as revised by the Savoy divines on the one side, and conformed to our Directory of Worship on the other. It alone would be a truly *Christian* liturgy, since it would be a formulated expression of the devotions of God's people as guided and illumined by the Holy Ghost in all ages of the Church; it alone would be a truly *Protestant* liturgy, since it would be freed from Mediæval or Roman errors and superstitions, and retain only such ancient formulas as are consistent with Primitive Christianity, together with the choicest formulas of the Reformation; and it alone would be a truly *Presbyterian* liturgy, since it would rest upon the authority of twenty orthodox divines, some of whom were among the framers of our Church standards, some of whom could have been bishops had they not preferred to remain presbyters and Presbyterians, and nearly all of whom maintained their Presbyterianism at a sacrifice of every worldly interest. We propose now to glance at the historical materials for such an edition, and the principles which should govern us in applying them.

"In the beginning of the blessed Reformation," said the framers of our Directory,* "our wise and pious ancestors took care to set forth an order for redress of many things which they then, by the Word, discovered to be vain, erroneous, superstitious, and idolatrous, in the public worship of God. This occasioned many godly and learned men to rejoice much at the Book of Common Prayer at that time set forth; because the mass, and the rest of the Latin service being removed, the public worship was celebrated in our own tongue. Many of the common people also received benefit by hearing the Scriptures read in their own language, which formerly were unto them as a book that is sealed.

"Howbeit long and sad experience hath made it manifest that the Liturgy used in the Church of England (notwithstanding all the pains and religious intentions of the compilers of it) hath proved an offence, not only to many of the godly at home, but also to the reformed Churches abroad."

---

* Preface to the Westminster Directory.

The history of the Prayer-book is indeed but the history of a struggle between evangelism and ritualism, spirituality and formality, in the Protestant Church of England. The successive revisions of the book were the pitched battles between the two parties, and the Savoy Conference was a last, decisive encounter, which marked the defeat on English soil of those Presbyterian principles which have since arisen and flourished without restraint in the Church of Scotland and in the churches of this country.

At the very dawn of the Reformation, these two tendencies began to show themselves. The first Prayer-book of King Edward VI., in 1549, had scarcely been issued before it was eagerly assailed by the more evangelical reformers, its relics of papal superstition expunged, and the whole thoroughly reviewed and amended. The result was King Edward's Second Book in 1552, by which the Calvinistic side of the Reformation got a firm foothold in the Church of England. The compilers and first revisers of the liturgy held to diocesan episcopacy simply as a convenient ancient institution which had been kept up in the Church "from the Apostles' time," and formed part of the existing organization of the State, a bishop being also a baron of the realm; and they not only recognised the parity of bishops and presbyters,* but invited foreign Presbyterian divines to occupy chairs of divinity in their universities, and to sit with them in a synod or council for the settlement of doctrine.† More than this; they actually consulted them, while the church service was undergoing reviewal, and drew largely from Presbyterian formularies which were then at hand and in use in the foreign congregations of Lasko and Pollanus. The introductory portions of the Daily Prayer

---

* Strype's Life of Cranmer, p. 420. Oxford edition; and similar opinions of Bishops Hooper, Jewel, Grindal, Parkhurst, Ponet, &c., in their writings collected by the Parker Society. They have been admirably collated in a series of articles in the *Episcopal Recorder*, Philadelphia, 1863.

† See Letters of Cranmer to Calvin, Bullinger, Melanchthon, Bucer, Lasco, and Hardenberg. Remains; Parker Society, pp. 420—434; Strype's Life of Cranmer, vol. i. pp. 280, 410.

and the Communion were the fruit, and still remain as the monuments, of this first revision.

The fortunes of the book are next to be traced to Frankfort on the Continent, whither it had been carried by the English Reformers in their flight from the persecutions of Queen Mary. John Knox was chosen one of the ministers to the congregation of exiles; and attempts were made, though not without some scandalous dissensions, at a further reformation of the Church ritual. Men who afterwards became eminent bishops in the English Church, at this time "gave up private baptisms, confirmation of children, saints' days, kneeling at the Holy Communion, the linen surplices of the ministers, crosses, and other things of the like character," retaining, however, "the remainder of the form of prayer and of the administration of the sacraments;" and "with the consent of the whole Church there was forthwith appointed one pastor, two preachers, four elders, two deacons; the greatest care being taken that every one should be at perfect liberty to vote as he pleased." Had these large concessions been properly represented to Calvin, to whom both parties appealed, it is fair to presume, he would have been more than satisfied with so near an approach to Presbyterian ideas of polity and worship.* But the controversy became embittered with personal and national antipathies; Knox and Whittingham, through the intrigue of their adversaries, were driven from Frankfort to Geneva, where they set up the Book of Common Order in antithesis to the Book of Common Prayer; and thus were sown the seeds of the great schism between the Church of England and the Church of Scotland.

Upon the accession of Queen Elizabeth in 1558, the exiles† were admitted to places of authority and influence

---

* Compare a "Brieff Discours off the troubles begonne at Frankford in Germany, A. D. 1554, Abowte the Booke off Common Prayer and Ceremonies," (reprinted London, 1845,) with the Letters addressed to Calvin by Cox, (afterwards Bishop of Ely,) Sandys, (Archbishop of York,) Grindal, (Archbishop of Canterbury,) &c. Original Letters, vol. ii. pp. 753—63. Parker Society edition.

† "Some of whom, during their absence, had been ordained according to the customs of the countries where they had resided

in the English Church, and, as might be expected, they came back prepared to urge the reforms which they had practised while abroad.* Such, at least, was the drift of their emendations, when occupied with the revision of the Prayer-book; but the compromising policy of Elizabeth, who had to deal with Romanists as well as Protestants, prevailed against the ecclesiastical commission,† and the liturgy, as re-established, leaned backward from the Second book of King Edward toward the First.

The great movement itself, however, still went forward. "The Genevan faction, or Puritan‡ party," as it is the fashion of certain writers to call them, began to issue modified editions of the Prayer-book, or in social worship to use Calvin's or Knox's liturgy, and even to form presbyteries within the Church establishment.§ And when King James ascended the throne in

---

These were admitted, without re-ordination, to preach and hold benefices. One of them (Whittingham) was promoted to a deanery." Bishop White's Essay on "The Case of the Episcopal Churches," page 22.

* Strype's Annals, vol. i., p. 127.

† "Except Archbishop Parker, who had remained in England during the late reign, and Cox, Bishop of Ely, who had taken a strong part at Frankfort against innovation, all the most eminent churchmen, such as Jewell, Grindal, Sandys, Noell, were in favour of leaving off the surplice, and what were called the Popish ceremonies. Whether their objections are to be deemed narrow and frivolous, or otherwise, it is inconsistent with veracity to dissemble that the Queen alone was the cause of retaining those observances to which the great separation from the Anglican establishment is ascribed." Hallam. Const. Hist. of England, chap. iv.

‡ The term Puritan was originally applied to all who sought greater *purity* in the Church, by freeing it from the remaining errors and superstitions of Romanism. The Presbyterian Puritans were from the first strict churchmen, agreeing with the Congregational Puritans in being Calvinists, but differing from them on questions of polity and liturgy. As they appeared "in the manor-houses of that old time, they were a stately, polite, religious people; not austere, yet not frivolous; whose theory of life was that the chief end of man is not to amuse and be amused, but to glorify God and enjoy him for ever." Bayne's Historical Introduction.

§ For a full account of the rise and spread of Presbyterianism in the Church of England, and its early and continued assertion of itself against Congregationalism on the one side, and Ritualism on the other, see the learned work of Professor Samuel Hopkins, "The Puritans and Queen Elizabeth," vol. i. chap. x., vol. ii. chaps. xv. xvi. Also Hetherington's History of the Westminster Divines, p. 43; Hodge's History of Pres. Church, chap. I.

1603, they had grown strong enough to present the famous "Millenary Petition," (so called because of its thousand signatures,) in which they renewed the objections first raised at Frankfort, praying "that the cross in baptism, interrogatories ministered to infants, confirmations, as superfluous, may be taken away; baptism not to be administered by women, and so explained; that examination may go before the communion; that it be ministered with a sermon; that divers terms of priests and absolution, and some other used, with the ring in marriage, and other such like in the book may be corrected; the longsomeness of service abridged; church songs and music moderated to better edification; that the Lord's day be not profaned; the rest upon holidays not so strictly urged; that there may be an uniformity of doctrine prescribed; no Popish opinion to be any more taught or defended; no ministers charged to teach their people to bow at the name of Jesus; and that the Canonical Scriptures only be read in church." And in view of this petition, it was deemed debatable by Archbishop Whitgift "whether to overthrow the said book, or to make alteration of things disliked in it." About this time also Lord Bacon published a pamphlet, in which, says Hallam, "he excepts to several matters of ceremony; the cap and surplice, the ring in marriage, the use of organs, the form of absolution, lay-baptism, &c." The result was that a Conference between the parties was appointed by King James at Hampton Court, and, after some discussion, several emendations made, which, if trivial, at least showed the steady growth of evangelical opinions.

While, however, Presbyterian divines were thus striving after a more primitive and Protestant worship, the opposite party were as steadily aiming at a semi-popish ritual, until at length, under the reign of Charles I., in 1637, the long pent storm burst forth. Archbishop Laud, with that passion for mediæval art which has since ensnared so many tasteful but narrow minds, began his ecclesiological experiments upon the Scots. Then followed the events described in our first chapters—the wild uprising of the Covenanters—their solemn League with the Puritans—the vain attempt by a new and more radical revision of the Prayer-book to stay the revolution—the defeat of Prelacy by the Parliamentary forces—the Assembly of Divines at Westminster—the Establishment of the Directory in place of the Liturgy—the rapid increase of the Independents—the overthrow of both Church and State in the time of the Commonwealth—the protest of the Presbyterian Clergy of London against the death of Charles the First and the crowning of Charles the Second, by the Scottish Presbyterians—the ultimate restoration of the Monarchy through their combined efforts and those of the Episcopalian Royalists—the re-action of Presbyterianism in favor of a revised Liturgy—its failure to effect a Reformation of the Prayer-book through the Savoy Conference*—and its final extinction by the Act of Uniformity.

Thus it appears that from the very origin of the Prayer-book, the spirit of English Presbyterianism had been steadily gaining ground with each successive revision, until at length it found itself between two extreme factions, one of which could see nothing good in the book, and the other nothing evil in it; and in the vain effort by turns to master and conciliate these hostile elements within the pale of an Established Church, it finally perished. But it died, only as the martyr dies, for the good of posterity. At the cost of its own life it restored monarchy to England, and gave democracy to America, and to the church universal bequeathed an amended Prayer-book, which, if it is still, as hitherto, to live only in history, must ever remain as the model of a pure, free, and catholic liturgy.

Now when we come to sift the literary materials which have accumulated during this exciting history, it will be found that, for our present purpose, we need make no account of any documents or writings before the last

---

* "The minds of the ruling Episcopalians, irritated by recent sufferings, were less intent on conciliation than on retaliation. Bishop Burnet assigns a reason still less excusable; that many great preferments were in the hands of obnoxious persons, who on account of their services towards the restoration, could not otherwise be ejected, than by making the terms of conformity difficult." Bishop White's Essay, p. 23.

revision in 1661; partly because it was not until that time that English Presbyterianism had fully unfolded and defined itself against Independency as well as Prelacy, and also because it then in fact gave a *resumé* (more thorough than any that could now be made,) of the previous Puritan revisions, together with its own matured exceptions and emendations. The records of the Savoy Conference alone, will yield us that expurgated Prayer-book which, in contrast with the Episcopalian editions now in use, shall express the sense of our standards on the authority, and to a great extent, in the very words of the learned divines who first framed and used them.

And happily, these invaluable records are not only full and explicit, but at length easily accessible.* It would be interesting to take them up in detail, and discuss them in their bearings upon the condition and prospects of modern Presbyterianism. But the question before us requires us only to select and present that one important document into which is collected the sense of all the others, and which must ever remain as the basis of anything deserving to be called a Presbyterian Liturgy.

A glance at the history† will show that the paper

---

* The Editor had been endeavoring to gather these papers from the obscure works in which they have hitherto been scattered, when his attention was called to a full collection of them, entitled "*Documents relating to the Settlement of the Church of England, by the Act of Uniformity of* 1662," a list of which will be found in our Appendix. The volume is issued by the "United Saint Bartholomew Committee," an organization formed in connection with the recent Bi Centenary Celebration of Non Conformity in London; and a Second Edition has a Historical Introduction by the distinguished Essayist, Peter Bayne. Esq., Editor of the *Weekly Review*, an Organ of the English Synod. The series of Documents, thus for the first time issued in a connected form, " exhibits the relations of the King, the Parliament, the Bishops, and the Presbyterian Divines to each other in the discussions which preceded and resulted in the Act of Uniformity:" and the Committee declare it was their "unanimous resolution that, in collecting them and presenting them to public notice, the most rigid impartiality should be observed." Their republication in our own country would shed much light into this greatly neglected department of our Church History.

† The fullest account may be found in Reliquiæ Baxterianæ, or Baxter's History of his own Life and Times, at first edited by Sylvester, and afterwards abridged by Calamy, (Chapter viii. London ed., 1713,) and by Orme, (vol. i. pp. 181—193, Boston ed, 1831.) Other

entitled "*The Exceptions against the Book of Common Prayer*," compiled by Reynolds, Wallis, Calamy, Newcomen, Bates, Clarke, Jacomb, &c., and presented at the opening of the Conference, is the only document which fully and authoritatively represents the views of the Presbyterian Commissioners. Other writings were indeed offered in their name, but not, as it would seem, with their full knowledge and sanction; this one being in fact the report of a committee to which had been assigned the duty of preparing the proposed "corrections and amendments," while the other papers, "The Petition for Peace and Concord presented to the Bishops with the proposed Reformation of the Liturgy," "The Rejoinder of the Ministers to the Answer of the Bishops," and "The Petition to the King at the close of the Conference," were of Baxter's composition alone, and brought forward at a stage of the proceedings when it had become plain that the Conference was a failure, and after several of the Presbyterians, among them Tuckney, had already left, in despair of any reconciliation. We make this discrimination merely to simplify our task; for the writings in question are not only deeply interesting as memorials of the time, but also exceedingly valuable for confirming and interpreting that chief document of the revision.

As to the production known as Baxter's "Reformed Liturgy," it should be observed, that it does not appear among the records,* and according to his statement, was not even read by the opposite party. It was in fact precluded by the terms of the King's Warrant, which extended only to "corrections, alterations, and amendments;" having been ingeniously so framed as to exclude the "additional forms" promised in the King's Declaration. Under this misapprehension, the task of preparing such supplementary forms would seem indeed to have been assigned to Baxter; but not, as has been absurdly charged, with the view of substitut-

---

sketches are given by Collier, Burnet, Neal, and various later writers, but they are mainly derived from Baxter's Narrative.

* It may be found in Calamy's Life of Baxter, vol. i., London ed., 1713. Also in Hall's Reliquiæ Liturgicæ.

ing them as a new liturgy in place of the Prayer-book. The real object aimed at was to secure freedom of worship, by the "addition or insertion of some other varying forms in Scripture phrase, to be used at the minister's choice,"* as well as to enrich the book with more Protestant models of devotion than the meagre versicles and collects of which it was then chiefly composed. Time may have shown that this scheme was impracticable, and set a lower estimate than his own upon Baxter's liturgical efforts; but the defect at which they were aimed was one which the Episcopalian Commissioners themselves afterward endeavored to supply, and which to this day is felt as a serious want by all who are accustomed to the freshness and variety of a less rigid mode of worship. It is a defect, however, which is only to be remedied by the grace of extemporaneous prayer; and the fate of Baxter's effusion should be a warning to every ambitious liturgy-maker not to think of legislating for that class of devotions which cannot, in the nature of the case, be formulated, but must be left to the pastor or bishop of each flock, as the mood or occasion will prompt him. Of all such rash attempts we may say what Milton said of the imposed Prayer-book: "To imprison and confine by force, within a pinfold of set words, those two most unimprisonable things, our prayers and that divine spirit of utterance that moves them, is a tyranny that would have longer hands than those giants who threatened bondage to heaven."†

Our present concern, therefore, is only with those ancient and catholic models which alone can properly enter into a free liturgy, and upon which alone the collective wisdom of the Presbyterian Commissioners was exercised. And no one can read their paper of corrections without being struck at once with its cautious and conservative tenor, and its entire harmony with the genius of Presbyterian worship. It yielded no small share of the emendations which distinguish the present Prayer-book‡ of the Church of England, and largely

---

* Documents, p. 17.
† Eikonoklastes, Chapter xvi., upon the Ordinance against the Common Prayer-book.
‡ Preface to the English Prayer-book.

accords with the exceptions which at this day are taken by the Liberal and Evangelical party. We may add, that whatever comparative excellences are to be found in the edition of the Protestant Episcopal Church in this country,* if not remotely derived from its suggestions, are at least in agreement with them. And yet it is, at the same time, so distinctive and unequivocal, in those parts which have hitherto been disregarded, that any sound Presbyterian of the present day will immediately recognise in it the work of the large-hearted men to whom we look as the founders and framers of our Church.

While, however, all this is true of the paper in general, yet it will be found that, in the actual work of applying it as in this edition, two abatements must be made in regard to such of its details as are confessedly of minor importance, and involve no question of doctrine or principle.

In the first place, it will be seen that the authors of the document themselves carefully discriminate between "some particulars that seem to be corrupt, and to carry in them a repugnancy to the rule of the Gospel," and "others dubious and disputable as not having a clear foundation in Scripture for their warrant," or still others "of inferior consideration, verbal rather than material, which, were they not in the public liturgy of so famous a church, we should not have mentioned." And that they would not have been tenacious of such points, had they been met by the other party with a spirit of amicable conference, is not only plain from the paper itself, (which was never designed as an *ultimatum*, being composed mainly of proposals and matters for treaty and consultation,) but was afterwards shown by their own concessions, when some of them, in the year 1698, under the reign of King William, united with Tillotson, Stillingfleet, Tennison, and other eminent Bishops, in a second attempt to revise the Liturgy with a view to their comprehension in the Church Establishment.† And though the effort again proved a failure,

---

* Preface, fourth paragraph, and p. 75 below.
† The MS. of the *Alterations in the Book of Common Prayer prepared by the Royal Commissioners for the Revision of the Liturgy in* 1689,

yet it has yielded us additional and most valuable helps, which we have not failed to use, in the interpretation and application of the document before us.

In the second place, it should be remembered that since this document was prepared, a great change has been steadily working in regard to many matters of mere usage and taste, involving no essential principle of Presbyterianism. The whole liturgical question, indeed, has meanwhile become reversed. Then it was the liberty to use the gift of prayer which was first to be asserted; now it is the liberty to use forms of prayer which is still to be preserved. It is obvious that many things which then were simply intolerable as parts of an enforced liturgy, may now be safely left indifferent under a directory, and that in thus consigning them to the spontaneous action of Christian feeling we are not abandoning, but only following out the principles of our forefathers, who craved no other freedom for themselves than they were willing to concede to their brethren.* Nor should it surprise us to find, after the lapse of two centuries, and in the altered circumstances in which we are now placed, that some of their minor criticisms seem trivial or inapplicable. This may only show what they themselves maintained, how impossible it is to make rules and forms for all cases, and also how invariable is that law of the human mind, by which it reacts from any extreme into which it has been driven.

---

after lying hidden under seal in Lambeth Library for more than a century and a half, became at length accessible, by order of Parliament, in the Blue Book of June 2d, 1854. An "Account of the proceedings of the Commissioners," and an Abstract of their proposed Emendations is given by Calamy in his Life of Baxter. Chapter xvii. Vol. i. A summary is also given in Procter's History of Prayer-book, p. 146, and the Revised Collects by Baird in the Book of Public Prayer. The *Alterations* have been largely used by Rev. Richard Bingham, in a late work entitled "*Liturgiæ Recusæ Exemplar:* the Prayer-book as it might be: or Formularies old, revised, and new, suggesting a reconstructed and amplified Liturgy," London, 1863.

* "We would avoid both the extreme that would have no forms, and the contrary extreme that would have nothing but forms. . . . It is a matter of far greater trouble to us, that you would deny us and all ministers the liberty of using any other prayers besides (the forms in) the liturgy than that you impose these." Rejoinder of the Presbyterians; Documents p. 247.

And yet, it would be a great mistake to suppose, because this paper was, in some trifling respects, originally defective, and in others has become obsolete, that therefore the editor has been thrown entirely upon his own taste and judgment, in applying it, or even in supplying its little deficiencies. We fortunately possess certain collateral sources of information, quite as authoritative and explicit, by means of which the two principal documents to be used may be fully confirmed and complemented even to the smallest particulars. What is wanting in the Savoy records, or in our Directory, is more than made up to us by other authorities cotemporary with the former, and cognate to the latter, so that not only upon all the great substantials of doctrine and order, but also upon the veriest minutiæ of usage, convenience, and taste, we can converge the light of history from every quarter.

If now we bring together and arrange the materials chiefly used in discriminating and preparing this edition, they may thus be exhibited at one view:

THE PRAYER-BOOK OF CHARLES I.

Presbyterian Exceptions of 1661.   *The Assembly's Directory.*
Presbyterian Rejoinder of 1661.   The Assembly's Digest.
Semi-Presbyterian Revision of 1689. The Calvinistic Liturgies.

THE PRESBYTERIAN PRAYER-BOOK.

It will be seen that the editor's task has been simply to take that edition which was in the hands of the Savoy Commissioners, and, in the first instance, apply to it the two documents which respectively represent the English and the American view of its contents; and his duty and aim have been to reject everything inconsistent with both, and retain all of either that remains. The text, therefore, or body of the service, has only been altered so far as the "Exceptions" require; but the Rubric has been everywhere superseded by the Directory, especially in the sacramental offices, in which it has been inserted literally. Thus the doctrinal framework has been taken from our standards, while the form and fashion of the whole have been rendered expressive of their import.

Then, as to the numerous details not reached by these two chief documents, we have used the auxiliary writings severally connected with them. For confirming and supplementing the Exceptions, we have compared Baxter's Rejoinder, which exhibits the Presbyterians at their farthest extreme from the Episcopalians,* and the Revision of 1689, which exhibits the Episcopalians in their nearest approach to the Presbyterians.† For confirming and supplementing the Directory, we have compared the Assembly's Acts and Deliverances, which present the most modern and American phase of Presbyterianism, and the Calvinistic or Reformed Liturgies, which present its most ancient and catholic aspect. And then the several products of these comparisons have been blended in the work of emendation, so far as consistent with each other and with the work as a whole. The result is, unless we greatly over-estimate our labors, a Prayer-book so amended as to contain nothing, however trivial, for which good Presbyterian authority and usage cannot be cited.

Having thus collected, sifted, and applied our materials, it only remains to analyze the product before us by tracing the several offices to their historical sources, and showing their fitness either as materials or models of divine worship. This we propose to do in our next chapter, leaving the reader, as we proceed, to compare the text with our commentary upon it.

---

* "All which considered, we altogether despair of that happy success which thousands hope and wait for from this his Majesty's commission; unless God shall incline your hearts for the peace and union of the nation, to a more considerable and satisfactory alteration of the liturgy." Calamy in the Presbyterian Rejoinder; Documents, p. 204.

† "Thus much I shall venture to say, that such Amendments as those were, with such an allowance in the point of Orders for Ordination by *Presbyters*, as is made 13 Eliz., cap. 12, would, in all probability, have brought in two-thirds of the Dissenters in England." Calamy, in his Life of Baxter, vol. 1. p. 448.

We have also made use of the "Proposals for a Comprehension of the Presbyterians," made by Stillingfleet and Tillotson in conference with Manton Bates and Baxter in 1668. Ibid. p. 317.

CHAPTER IX.

HISTORICAL AND CRITICAL ANALYSIS OF THE AMENDED PRESBYTERIAN PRAYER-BOOK.

As the object we have in view does not take us over the ancient ground common to all Liturgies and Prayer-books, and already pre-occupied by so many learned treatises,* we shall confine ourselves mainly to such investigations as may serve to distinguish this edition from others; and our method will be to penetrate first to the original sources from which the book was compiled, and then, by a more specific criticism of its contents, to trace the changes through which it has passed to its present amended form, together with the reasons active in producing them.

SECT. I. *The Catholic Originals.*

In the early progress of the Reformation, royal injunctions were given that certain portions of the Latin service, then used in the churches, such as the Lord's Prayer, the Creed, and the Epistle and Gospel for the day, should be recited from the pulpit in the mother tongue; that the English Litany should be said plainly by the priest and choir in the midst of the church; and that after matins should be read a Lesson from the New Testament, and after evensong a Lesson from the Old Testament.† At the same time an "Order of Communion" was issued, restoring the cup to the laity, and virtually abolishing the Roman Mass;‡ and

---

* Palmer: *Origines Liturgicæ.* Bingham: *Origines Ecclesiasticæ.* Maskel: *Monumenta Ritualia Ecclesiæ Anglicanæ.* Freeman: *Principles of Divine Service.*
† Injunctions given by the most Excellent Prince, Edward the Sixth, &c. Appendix to Archbishop Cranmer's Remains, p. 498. Parker Society ed.
‡ Liturgies of King Edward the Sixth, pp. 1—8, Parker Society edition.

at length these several elements of a Protestant liturgy became embodied in a "Book of Common Prayer," designed to supersede the old monastic ritual, and engage the whole people intelligently in every part of divine service.*

The nucleus of the Prayer-book was thus immediately derived from the Breviary and Missal, as translated by the English Reformers, and adapted to the uses of congregational worship: but remotely it was of much more primitive and less questionable origin; and, as here presented, after all the revisions it has undergone, with its numerous Protestant accretions, erasions, and emendations, it will be found to retain scarcely a trace of the Roman and Anglican channels through which it has passed from its ancient sources, and to be indeed, so far as it is not distinctively Presbyterian, simply catholic or common to all churches of Christ.

Leaving this fact to appear as we proceed, we pass to those more modern originals concerning which there is greater diversity of opinion.

Sect. II. *The Protestant Originals.*

Besides the ancient service-books there were also in the hands of the compilers of the Prayer-book three new formularies, portions of which were incorporated in the first and second editions. These were, 1. Hermann's Consultation or scheme of doctrine and worship for the Electorate of Cologne. 2. Pollanus's Liturgy of the Church of French Refugees in England. 3. Lasco's Ecclesiastical Service of the Church of German Foreigners in London. It is important to discriminate the sources from which these formularies had been compiled, and the changes they underwent both before and after they were embodied in the English liturgy.

As to the origin of the two last named productions there can be no question. It is conceded by all parties, that they were translated from a form which had been composed and used by Calvin in the church at Stras-

---

* Preface to the Book of Common Prayer, 1549, Strype, vol. ii p. 133.

burg, and which became the germ and model of all the Reformed liturgies.* This is clear not only from their structure and contents, but also from the events connected with their origin and history.

Valerandus Pollanus was Calvin's successor at Strasburg, and on the publication of the Interim, an imperial edict adverse to the Reformers, fled with his congregation to England, where the Lord Protector gave them an asylum in Somersetshire, and allowed them the free use of their ritual in Glastonbury Cathedral. The disputes in the English church which led to the further reformation and amendment of the Prayer-book, turned the attention of both parties to these foreign Protestants, and Pollanus in 1550–51, published in Latin, Calvin's Strasburg liturgy as used by them, together with a Dedication to King Edward the Sixth, and an Apology, vindicating them from the aspersions of the Romanists.†

---

* This must not be confounded with Calvin's Genevan Liturgy, which differed from the Strasburg in some of the respects in which the latter agreed, with the Prayer-book. Eutaxia, p. 20, 206.

The following authorities, representing all varieties of theological prepossession, may be consulted in regard to the Calvinistic originals of the Prayer-book:

(*Anglican.*) History of the Prayer-book, by Archdeacon Berens, published by the Society for Promoting Christian Knowledge, pages 39, 41, 43, 87, 88, 141, 155—8; Archbishop Laurence's Bampton Lectures, pages 207, 208; Freeman's "Principles of Divine Service," vol. i., p. 313; Procter's History of the Prayer-book, pages 31. 32, 45—49, 341, 346, note; "Private Prayers in the Reign of Queen Elizabeth;" Parker Society, p. 488, note; Strype's Eccl. Mem. vol. ii., chapter xxix.; Burnet's History of the Reformation. p. 415; Strype's Life of Cranmer, p. 200, and Appendix; Heylin's History of the Reformation, published by the Eccl. Hist. Society, vol. i. pages 193, 226, 270; Hardwicke's History of the Christian Church during the Reformation, Cambridge edition, pages 222, 223.

(*German.*) Daniel's Codex Liturgicus; Eccl. Ref. et Angl., vol. i; Ebrard's Reformirtes Kirchenbuch, p. 323; Hertzog's Encyclopedia. Articles: England, Anglican Church, Cranmer, and Calvin.

(*American.*) Bishop Brownel's Commentary on the Prayer book, Introduction, p 21. Eutaxia or the Presbyterian Liturgies, chapters x—xii. Mr. Baird's careful researches into the Calvinistic Liturgies place his work in the first rank of authorities.

† *Liturgia Sacra, Seu Ritus Ministerii in Ecclesia Peregrinorum Profugorum propter Evangelium Christi Argentinæ.* 1551. *Cum Apologia pro hac Liturgia. Per Valerandum Pollanum Flandrum.* The date is incorrectly given by Proctor. Compare with Strype, vol. ii. 379. It may be found in Daniel's Codex Liturgicus, vol. 1.

About the same time a distinguished Pole, John A. Lasco, also a Calvinist, or Zwinglian, took shelter in England upon the invitation of Cranmer, and was appointed superintendent of the foreign congregation of refugees in London. The liturgy used in their worship, was prepared by him on the basis of that translated by Pollanus, and was published both in Dutch and in Latin.* Lasco, moreover, was intimately associated with Cranmer, as his guest and adviser, while the liturgy was undergoing revision, and took an active part in the whole work of the English Reformation.

It is thus evident from the history, that the Calvinistic liturgy was not only in actual use in several congregations to which the framers of the Prayer-book would naturally refer for an example of Protestant worship but that it was also in their hands in several languages. And this historical testimony, as we shall see hereafter, is amply sustained by the internal evidence of the book itself.

In regard to the other work mentioned, that of Bucer and Melancthon, there is more room for doubt.† It

---

* *Forma ac Ratio tota ecclesiastici ministerii in peregrinorum, potissimum vero Germanorum Ecclesia instituta Londini in Anglia per Edvardum Sextum.* Auctore Joh. A. Lasco, Poloniæ Barne. Both Lasco's and Pollanus' Liturgies are sketched by Dr. Krauth in his "Sunday Service according to the Liturgies of the Churches of the Reformation."

† This work was not so much a liturgy as a provisional scheme of doctrine and worship, which Melancthon and Bucer were invited to prepare by Hermann, "that pious Confessor the late Elector and Archbishop of Cologne, who, for adhering to the Protestant religion, and setting on foot the Reformation of his country, was deprived by the Pope and Emperor." It was first published in German in 1543, and in 1545 in Latin at Donn. with the title, "*Nostra Hermanni Archepisc. Coloniensis Simplex et Pia Deliberatio et Christiana in Verbo Dei fundata Reformatio.*" An English translation of this Latin work was printed in 1547, and a second revised edition in 1548, entitled, "A simple and religious consultation of us Hermann, by the grace of God, Archbishop of Cologne, and Prince Elector, &c., by what means a Christian Reformation, and founded in God's word, of doctrine, administration of the divine Sacraments, of ceremonies, and the whole cure of souls, and other ecclesiastical ministries, may be begun among men committed to our pastoral charge, until the Lord grant a better to be appointed either by a free and Christian council, general or national, or else by the States of the Empire of Germany, gathered together in the Holy Ghost." Procter's History

would, in fact, be simply absurd for any party now to lay an exclusive claim to the authorship or purport of a production which was compiled by divines noted for liberal views and union tendencies, and with the express design of reconciling the two extremes of the Reformation. After investigating the history in all directions, and viewing the question on all sides, we have reached the conclusion that, as this liturgy started at some middle-point between Lutheranism and Zwinglianism, it therefore entered the Prayer-book with a bias toward Calvinism, and that this bias was confirmed at the first revision, increased at each succeeding revision, and finally completed by the Presbyterian Commissioners at the last revision. Our reasons for this view are the following:

1. It was never used or sanctioned in any Lutheran community, but on the contrary, was opposed and suppressed by Luther himself on its first appearance.*

2. Not only was it compiled from Reformed as well as Lutheran sources,† but both of its compilers were warm personal friends of Calvin, and favorable to a union

---

of the Prayer-book, p. 40. The Cologne Liturgy is noticed in Strype's Ecc. Mem., and the German edition of it may be found in Richter's Kirchenordnungen. vol. i.

* "The Reformation Book, which was mainly Bucer's work, and in which, so far as the liturgy is concerned, the established ritual was followed as closely as possible, the Constitution of the Church retained, and the doctrine of the Strasburg and Hessian Confessions adopted—was sent by Hermann himself to the Elector of Saxony, who submitted it for examination to the Lutheran zealot Ormsdorf. Luther was incensed by it, especially in regard to the Lord's Supper, and first assailed Bucer, and became so much excited against Melancthon, that the latter thought seriously of leaving Wittemberg, expecting that Luther would come out publicly against him." Life of Bucer, by J. W. Baum, Prof in Strasburg, p. 535.

† From the formularies of Nuremburg (Lutheran,); Saxony (Lutheran,); Strasburg (Reformed,) and Hesse (Reformed.) See Richter's Evangelischen Kirchenordnungen, vol. i.

It appears from a letter of Melancthon that the doctrinal portion was prepared by himself, while the ritual portion, (which is the part that appears in the Prayer-book.) was prepared by Bucer. "Retinuit pleraque Osiandri Bucerus; quosdam articulos auxit, ut est copiosus. Mihi, cum omnia relegissem, attribuit articulos, de trinitate, de creatione, de peccato originis, de justitia fidei et operum, de ecclesia, de pœnitentia. In his consumpsi tempus hactenus, et legi de cæremoniis Baptismi et Cœnæ Domini quæ ipse composuit." Epist. 2707 Opp. v. 112.

with the Calvinistic churches.* This feeling, indeed, in Bucer amounted to a ruling passion, drew upon him the suspicion and persecution of his countrymen, and at length forced him into exile and poverty. Calvin was the first to offer him an asylum at Geneva, but afterwards advised him to accept Cranmer's invitation to a professorship in Oxford, and addressed him a letter full of the highest consolations of Christian philosophy.†

3. Whatever may be said of Bucer's seeming inconsistency and vacillation in Germany, or of the syncretistic nature of the liturgy he there compiled, yet it is undeniable that while he was in England, assisting in the revision of the Prayer-book, he represented the views of Calvin, who had written him urging that "all ceremonies may be abolished which in any way savour of superstition,"‡ and who often mourned his untimely death as the greatest calamity to the English Reformation. "When I consider what a loss the Church of God has suffered by the death of this one man, I cannot but every now and then renew my grief. He would have done great service in England; and I hoped for something greater from his writings hereafter than what he has hitherto published."§ And that these hopes‖ had been well founded is shown by the strictures or *censura* of the Prayer-book,¶ which Bucer prepared at the

---

* See Calvin's Tracts, vol. ii. pp. 211, 281, 354—356, 496; Calvin's Letters, vol. i. p. 137; Zurich Letters, First Series, pp. 161, 234; Second Series, p. 73; Original Letters of Ref. pp. 488, 535, 544—548, 585, 688. Published by Parker Society. Strype's Ecc. Mem., vol. ii. pp. 190, 326. Hertzog's Encyclodedia, Art. Bucer, and Calvin.
† Calvin's Letters, trans. by Jules Bonnet, vol. ii. p. 212.
‡ Ibid. p. 232.   § Ibid. p. 312.
‖ Milton calls Bucer "that elect instrument of reformation highly honored, and had in reverence by Edward the Sixth and his whole Parliament" . . . "whose incomparable youth doubtless had brought forth to the Church of England such a glorious manhood, had his life reached it, as would have left in the affairs of religion nothing without an excellent pattern for us now to follow." Prose Works, Bohn's edition, pp. 317, 278. See also Milton's collection of "Testimonies of the high approbation which learned men have given of Martin Bucer." pp. 274—277.
¶ *Censura Martini Buceri super libro Sacrorum, seu ordinationis ecclesiæ atque ministerii ecclesiastici in Regno Angliæ, ad petitionem R. Archiepiscopi Cantuariensis, Thomæ Cranmeri conscripta.* A summary of the *Censura* is given by Procter, pages 40—43.

request of Cranmer, and which are in fact almost identical with those afterwards urged by the Calvinistic party in the Church of England.

4. Had the Bucerian and Melancthonian portions of the Prayer-book been thus amended according to Bucer's own matured views and suggestions, they would have been rendered almost entirely Calvinistic, and the English Church, in ritual as well as doctrine, would have been freed from its Romanist and Lutheran remnants.* But it was reserved for the Puritans, during the hundred years which followed, to continue the work of criticism begun by the Calvinistic reformers, and at length for the Presbyterian Puritans, in distinction from the Episcopalian Puritans on the one side, and the Independent Puritans on the other, to complete that work by their strictures offered in the Savoy Conference. "The Exceptions against the Book of Common Prayer" are at once a *résumé* and enlargement of the "Censura super Libro Sacrorum;" and the two documents, taken together, mark the germ and the flower of a Prayer-book that deserves in every sense to be called Presbyterian.

If now we survey the originals of the English Liturgy, at one view, from their origin throughout their history, we shall be ready for the general conclusion; that, while King Edward's First Prayer-book exhibited the Protestant as distinguished from the Romanist phase of Christianity, and while King Edward's Second Prayer-book exhibited the Calvinistic as distinguished from the Lutheran phase of Protestantism, the Prayer-book here presented will exhibit the Presbyterian as distinguished from the Episcopalian phase of Calvinism. And the proofs of this will accumulate at every step of that more particular analysis to which we proceed.

SECT. III. *The Revised Rubrics.*

The *Rubrics* (so called from the red letters in which they were printed in old copies) are the rules for the

---

* "The death of Edward seems to have prevented a further approach to the scheme of Geneva in our ceremonies, and perhaps in our Church government." Hallam's Const. Hist., chap. iv.

government of Minister and People in Divine Service, and correspond to our Directory. In the ancient Service-books, as well as in the Lutheran and Reformed *Agenda*, they are much less imperative and obligatory than in the English Prayer-book, which breathes throughout a tone of punctilious command, better suited to a state ritual than a church service. This has been obviated by substituting in place of the word "*shall*" the word "*will*" to indicate what is agreed and customary, or the word "*may*" to indicate what is discretionary and variable: a change which simply gains liberty without sacrificing order, since custom soon acquires the force of authority, and authority is of no avail where it loses its hold upon custom, as is shown by the continual conflict of usage with Rubrics and Directories.

The Introductory rubrics concerning ecclesiastical vestments and furniture, are ommitted as relating to matters which by the Directory are wisely and safely left indifferent. The *altar*,* and *surplice*,† were associated in the minds of many Episcopalians, as well as Presbyterians, with a false doctrine of the ministry and sacraments, and are at best but a poor imitation of the significant ritual in which they originated. The simplicity and spirituality of Christian worship would seem better represented and promoted by those traditional symbols of Presbyterianism, the pulpit, the communion-table, the baptismal font, and (if anything more official than the ordinary clerical dress is desired) the Genevan robes, customary in the Dutch churches or the scholar's gown, still in use in some of our own pulpits.

For similar reasons the rubrics concerning behaviour have been expunged, except in the few instances where

---

* Cranmer's "Six Reasons why the Lord's Board should rather be after the form of a Table than of an Altar." Remains and Letters, p. 524. Similar opinions were maintained by Bishops Ridley, Hooper, &c.

† Bishop Jewel pronounced it "a stage dress, a fool's coat, a relique of the Amorites." Archbishop Grindal "hesitated about accepting a mitre from dislike of what he called the mummery of consecration," and together with Bishops Sandys and Noel, was "in favor of leaving off the surplice." In these views Bucer and Martyr concurred. Zurich Letters, 161; Original Letters of Ref., 488, 585. Strype's Ecc. Mem., chap. xxviii; and Life of Cranmer, vol. ii. p. 210;

some direction seemed needful, and not likely to trench upon existing usage or liberty. The genuflexions, intonations, and bowings, practised in the English ritual, were desired by our forefathers to be left free to each worshipper, because of a feeling that nothing is so abhorrent in the sight of both God and man, as a devout demeanor, which is either enforced or simulated. The Book as here amended may be used either by the minister alone, or by the congregation with him, when both are so agreed; the minister leading in the whole service audibly, and the congregation accompanying him with the heart or with the voice also, in those parts marked as more especially assigned to them, according as each one's devotion shall prompt him. It should be said, however, that the actual reading of divine service by the parties, is a species of pupilage, to be endured only until they have become so familiar with it as to be able to say it from the heart without any danger of saying it only from the book.

As to *responses*, except where personal feeling is strong enough to impel them above the low tone of ordinary devotion, we may urge the objection, brought against them two hundred years ago, that "they cause a confused murmur in the congregation, whereby what is read is less intelligible and therefore unedifying;"* and the difficulty, always encountered of making them general and accordant, renders them on grounds of taste as well as of devotion, unsuitable to a mixed assembly. They properly belong in fact to the choral or monastic service from which they were borrowed, and in which they were artistically rendered by trained worshippers, and in a Protestant Church must cease to be expressive precisely in proportion as they become impressive.

As to *posture*, we only remark in general, that while standing and kneeling are both of them scriptural attitudes in prayer, and alike sanctioned by catholic and Presbyterian usage† yet in using these services it will

---

* Presbyterian "Exceptions." No. iii. See Appendix, and Eutaxia, page 27.
† " To pray standing, was in public worship believed to have been an Apostolic usage. The Presbyterians of Scotland, and at times the

be most convenient for the worshipper to bow the head or the knee in the Prayers and Confessions, to stand up in the Creeds, Psalms, Hymns and Doxologies, and to remain seated during Lessons, Exhortations, and Sermons.

In nothing is the rigidity and bondage of an imposed Prayer-book so manifest as in the mode of combining, or rather aggregating together the several offices it prescribes. According to the theory of those offices, the Lord's day would be marked by a succession of distinct services each complete in itself, and performed at different hours; beginning with Morning Prayer at dawn, and ending with Evening Prayer at twilight, with the Litany, Sermon, and Communion, intervening towards mid-day as the distinguishing or proper services of the day. Instead of crudely joining all of these together in a single morning service, full of needless repetitions and a tedious prolixity of parts, it would seem more reasonable to use each, as originally designed, separately, or at least to combine them with some discretion. It will be found, by following the rubric as amended, that without any perplexity to either party, the minister may practise either of the following six varieties of devotional service before the Sermon or Communion:

1. Morning Prayer.
2. Litany.
3. Sunday Service.
4. Morning Prayer and Litany.
5. Litany and Sunday Service.
6. Sunday Service and Litany.

A principal section of one office might also be conjoined to that of another, by proceeding as far as the

---

Lutherans of Germany, are probably the only occidental Christians who now observe the one only rubric laid down for Christian worship by the first Œcumenical Council." Stanley's Eastern Church, page 263. The Direction in Pollanus' Liturgy is "Ac toto hoc tempore (during Confession and Absolution,) populus magna cum reverentia vel astat, vel procumbit in genua, utut animus cujusque tulerit." Posture in the Daily service was prescribed only in the Creed and Confession, until the last revision. In the Communion, kneeling was prescribed, but according to I. and II. Edward. it was to "be used or left as every man's devotion serveth, without blame." See Documents, p. 131. Among the Proposals of 1689, was one, "That if any refuse to receive the Sacrament of the Lord's Supper kneeling, it may be administered to them in their pews." Calamy, p. 453. In the Church of Calvin the communicants came forward by groups to receive the elements. Eutaxia, p. 45.

First Lesson, and then beginning the Lord's day service (Ante-Communion,) or by proceeding as far as the Second Lesson, and then beginning the Epistle and Gospel for the day, (or Proper Service,) according to either of the following conjunctions:

    First Lesson.   Te Deum.
    Collect and Commandments.   or   Epistle and Gospel.
    Collect, Epistle, and Gospel.   Beatitudes.

This arrangement would not only obviate the repetitious use of Lessons, as well as Creeds, but also afford the means of adapting the service to the church-season by omitting either the Commandments, or the Te Deum, according to the nature of the occasion; and it ought not to disturb a liturgical purist, as much as the patchwork of inserting the Communion-Absolution, Creed, and Gloria in Excelsis, in the midst of the Daily Prayer.

The use of some such discretion as to omissions or variations, will be the more needful if any of the Occasional services are to be introduced, or if the circumstances are so extraordinary as to require a modification of the whole service. The Presbyterian revisers were surely not hypercritical, when they questioned whether it did not savor of "vain repetition," for even the Lord's prayer to be said six times,[*] by the same assembly; and that they were neither factious nor eccentric in craving for the minister the judicious " use of those gifts for prayer and exhortation, which Christ hath given him for the service and edification of the church, according to its various and emergent necessity,"[†] is shown by the fact that we have lived to see Episcopalian *Prayer-meetings* in advance of Presbyterian *Prayer-books*.

SECT. IV. *The Revised Daily Services.*

In all the Reformed Churches it was the custom to have Daily Prayers,[‡] morning and evening, at church as well as at home, in distinction from those of Roman-

---

[*] Documents, &c., p. 124, 306.   [†] Ibid. p. 17, 115.
[‡] Calvin's Daily Offices. Eutaxia, chap. iii.

ism, which were monastic, rather than congregational or domestic; and when the Latin was superseded by the English service, the Versicles, Collects, Canticles, and Creeds, which had been hitherto confined to the priest and choir, were transferred in the form of *Common Prayers* to the whole worshipping assembly. "The history of the English church tells of ceaseless endeavors to make these services in practice what they were in theory, the ritual of the whole body of the faithful. But the seven-fold nature of the scheme on which they were framed, and withal their unvernacular shape, forbad the possibility of any such use of them."* They are in fact the least Protestant portions of the Prayer-book, and are not to be found in any of the Reformed Liturgies, though as here presented, it will be seen that they have been comparatively freed from the objections mentioned.

The Order for Daily Prayer may be conveniently considered in three parts, 1. the introduction, consisting of the Sentences, Exhortation, Confession, and Absolution; 2. the body of the service, consisting of the Lord's Prayer, Gloria Patri, Psalmody, Lessons, Creed, and Collects; and 3. the conclusion, consisting of the Prayers, Thanksgivings, and Benediction. We shall find that of these several parts, the first and third are of Presbyterian origin, while the intermediate portion, after the Presbyterian revisions through which it has passed, retains scarcely anything Roman or Anglican.

(I.) "The truth respecting the very appropriate opening of our service seems to be," says Procter, "that the hint was taken from two books of service, used by congregations of refugees in England, which were published about this time: the one being the version of Calvin's form by Pollanus; and the other that used by the Walloons under John A. Lasco." The idea of such a penitential introduction, to take the place of private confession and absolution, was due to Calvin, and its whole structure is obviously Protestant, popular, and at variance with mediæval models.† It therefore

---

* Freeman as quoted by Procter.
† Compare the *Confiteor* with any Reformed Confession.

appears in the Prayer-book, prefixed to the Morning Prayer, and is not found in the first edition, nor printed before the Evening Prayer until the last edition.*

The *Sentences* form the basis of the Exhortation, and are sundry texts of Scripture designed to move to the Confession and prepare for the Absolution. In the Morning Prayer, they have been retained without change, as found in the English edition; but in the Evening Prayer others have been added, for alternative use, of a more various import, compiled from different Reformed Liturgies.

The *Exhortation* inculcates the need of Confession and Absolution, or penitence and pardon, as preliminary to the acts of thanksgiving, praise, hearing of God's Word, and prayer, which are announced as to follow in the body of the service. It was evidently modelled upon similar forms, common in all the Reformed Churches, and is eminently applicable to a congregation emerging into the light of Protestant worship, or to a congregation needing instruction in the elements of such worship, or to any congregation as a weekly or occasional exhortation, but its use twice every day would be but one of the inconsistencies of a liturgy that allows no discretion.

The *Confession* follows as the act of the congregation, incited to repentance by the Sentences and Exhortation, and is necessarily *general* in its terms, though not originally designed to preclude more particular confession, which might be silently made during a brief pause at the close. It was derived from the Calvinistic models of Pollanus and Lasco, but is English, and more scriptural in style, and less doctrinal in its import. Its supposed want of an explicit acknowledgment of original as well as actual sin was denied by the Episcopalians,† is still scrupled by Unitarians,‡ and, if originally

---

* Compare *Breviarium Romanum*, King Edward's First Prayer-book and Primer, and the present English Prayer-book.

† Answer of the Bishops; Documents, p. 115; Burnet's Hist. of the Ref., p. 415.

‡ Compare Common Prayer for Christian Worship, edited by Rev. James Martineau, and the Book of Common Prayer according to the use of King's Chapel, Boston, in both of which the phrase, "there is no health in us," is omitted.

intended, could not have been significant in a book that elsewhere abounds in assertions of that doctrine. Such dogmatic confessions, indeed, would seem rather to befit some later stage of the service than its beginning; and however valuable and essential they may be in their proper place, it would certainly be a rash hand that, for the sake of them, would now mar this time-hallowed formula.

The *Absolution (or Remission of Sins*, as the title was amended after the Hampton revision, in deference to Puritan scruples against a word of popish sound) ensues upon the Confession as the act of the Minister speaking to the people in the name and by the authority of Christ. It differs from other official declarations of divine grace only in being more formal and in deriving peculiar solemnity from its connection with an act of public devotion. Such a formula is found in all the Calvinistic liturgies except the Genevan, from which it was excluded by a scruple. "There is none of us," says Calvin, "but must acknowledge it to be very useful that, after the General Confession, some striking promise of Scripture should follow, whereby sinners might be raised to the hopes of pardon and reconciliation. And I would have introduced this custom from the beginning, but some fearing the novelty of it would give offence, I was over easy in yielding to them;* so the thing was omitted, and now it would not be seasonable to make any change, because the greatest part of our people begin to rise up before we come to the end of the Confession." In most of the Reformed Churches, the Absolution was variable in form, consisting simply of "some striking promise of Scripture," pronounced by the minister, like the "Comfortable Words" after the Confession in the Communion service; but in Lasco's liturgy, from which the Prayer-book version was taken,† it had assumed a more liturgical, though

---

* It was, however, adopted, through his advice in other Reformed Churches, and especially incorporated in his Strasburg liturgy, which his disciple and successor Pollanus introduced into England, and upon the basis of which Lasco's Service-book was framed.

† "In this book, (Lasco's,)" says Procter, "there is a form of Confession and of Absolution, in which some phrases resemble the cor-

less scriptural style. The petition, or mutual intercession of minister and people, with which it concludes, (unhappily turned into an exhortation in late editions, but in this preserved literally,) gathers up the purport of the whole preceding service as preparatory to that which is to follow, and so meets a want felt by the Presbyterian revisionists.*

(II.) At this point we leave the modern, and enter upon the ancient portion of the office; and that which forms our second general division. It consists mainly of Psalms and Lessons, those catholic elements of all worship, both Hebrew and Christian, Romanist and Protestant, but is peculiar in admitting a responsive element more largely than any other congregational liturgy; a peculiarity due to its monastic origin, and here modified by the Presbyterian emendations.

The Lord's Prayer, with which it begins, fittingly enters the service as that divine model and rule,† it ever behoves us to use, "when we pray." In the Latin ritual, it had been said secretly by the Priest alone, the Choir responding as he raised his voice in the concluding petition; but afterwards it was said aloud by the minister, and since the last revision, by both minister and people. The *doxology* with which it closes, was added at the instance of the Presbyterians,‡ is scriptural, in accordance with Greek as distinguished from Roman usage, and appropriately connects the preced-

---

responding portions which were added to the Second Book of King Edward VI. 'Neque amplius velis mortem peccatoris, sed potius ut convertatur et vivat . . . omnibus vere pœnitentibus (qui videlicet agnitis pecatis suis cum sui accusatione gratiam ipsius per nomen Christi Domini implorant) omnia ipsorum peccata prorsus condonet atque aboleat . . . omnibus, inquam, vobis qui ita affecti, estis denuncio, fiducia promissionum Christi, vestra peccata omnia in cœlo a Deo Patre nostro modis plane omnibus remissa esse . . . opem tuam divinam per meritum Filii tui dilecti supplices implorumus .. nobisque dones Spiritum Sanctum tuum . . . ut lex tua sancti illi (cordi) insculpi ac per nos demum . . . tota vita nostra exprimi ejus beneficio possit.'"

* Exception XVII.
† Larger Catechism, p. 187. Westminster Directory. Public Prayer.
‡ Exceptions. See Appendix.

ing act of penitence with the following office of praise and psalmody.

In the edition which was before the Savoy Commissioners, certain *Versicles* taken from the ancient service, were then added as follows:

> *Minister.* O Lord, open thou our lips,
> *Answer.* And our mouth shall show forth thy praise.
> *Minister.* O God, make speed to save us,
> *Answer.* O God, make haste to help us.
> *Minister.* Glory be to the Father, and to the, &c.,
> As it was in the beginning, is now, &c.
> Praise ye the Lord.

In accordance with the Presbyterian Exceptions,* we have retained only so much of this portion as seems needful to mark the transition of the service, and in a form neither requiring, nor precluding the responses. The second couplet in fact breaks the sense and is easily spared, but the *Gloria Patri,* which is a Trinitarian doxology of primitive origin and Presbyterian sanction,† is certainly appropriate to the worshipper, rising from confession, absolution, and prayer, to engage in praise. After the minister's invitation, *Praise ye the Lord,* an additional response, "The Lord's name be praised," was interpolated, by Laud,‡ in the Scottish Prayer-book of 1637, and is still found in late editions.

The *Venite Exultemus,*§ or 95th Psalm, had been sung from an early period, as introductory either to the whole service, or to the psalmody immediately following it; and for ordinary occasions there could certainly be no Psalm more appropriate; but there may be times when discretion will suggest some other selection, both here and also at the opening of the Evening Prayer, where another example is given.

After the Venite comes the daily portion of the *Psalter,* which, according to mediæval usage, was sung

---

* Exception III.
† Rejoinder. Documents, pp. 210, 295. According to Bellarmine it was "formed in the Council of Nicæa, as a particular testimony against the Arians."
‡ Proctor's Hist. of Prayer-book, p. 213.
§ The Latin titles, which are remnants of the ancient service, are the first phrase or words of the Psalm or Hymn to which they refer.

through in course once every week, and for this purpose divided into seven parts called nocturns; but in the reformed service was appointed to be read through once every month, a change which has the advantage of bringing the whole Book of Psalms into the Sunday Service, though not in their inspired order. It may be questioned, therefore, whether a yearly course of the Psalms, arranged for the Lord's day alone, would not secure a more orderly acquaintance with them, in view of modern usage as to daily services; and such an arrangement may be found in one of the Tables.

The *responsive reading* of the verses by minister and people may have been a rude substitute for the antiphonal chanting of priest and choir; but it is open to the objection already urged against all unmusical responses; it is in violation of the sense or rhythm which is often parallelistic in the members of each verse, rather than by alternate verses;* and, except for habituated nerves, is even less solemn than the doggerel of Rouse, or Watts unequally yoked with worldly airs. The experience of the whole Church would seem to be fast settling towards the conviction that the Psalms cannot with propriety be either versified or read, but should be simply chanted in prose,† according to their original structure in the temple-service, and the usage of catholic antiquity. In such a view, the extremes of doctrine and culture may meet, the most conscientious advocacy of literal psalmody be reconciled to the highest style of musical art, and the vexed relations of choir and congregation harmoniously adjusted. And it is this class of considerations which has mainly influenced us in here retaining the older version of the Psalter. It is more Calvinistic in origin, and more Saxon in style, than the approved translation;‡ and

---

* Tholuck on the Psalms; Introduction. Sect. ii. Hengstenberg on the Psalms; Appendix. The Formal Arrangement of the Psalms.

† Assembly's Digest; Psalmody.

‡ The Prayer-book Psalter was derived from several German and Latin versions as translated into English and afterwards twice revised by Coverdale, "a zealous Calvinist, both in doctrine and discipline," who, together with Whittingham, Knox, Pollanus, and

though not to be compared with it for didactic purposes when read as the rest of holy Scripture in lessons, yet it is certainly quite as "smooth and fit for song" as any metrical version, and has the advantage of having been long in use, and of being already pointed as it is to be sung; the colon (:) in each verse marking the division of the chant, throughout the Psalter, as in all the other musical portions of this edition.

The *repetition of the Gloria Patri* after each Psalm was questioned by the Presbyterians as a somewhat mechanical performance; is not in accordance with the most catholic usage, and after some Psalms is evidently unsuitable; but its use at the close of the psalmody may serve to Christianize the Hebrew lyrics, and would seem to be a fitting climax to the act of praise, especially when, upon its first occurrence, it has been said rather than sung.

We next enter upon the didactic part of the office, the *Reading of the Scriptures*, which is assigned exclusively to the Minister of the Word, and fitly follows the congregational acts of confession and psalmody, as that "part of the public worship of God wherein we acknowledge our dependence upon him, and subjection to him, and one means sanctified by him for the edifying of his people."* Before the Reformation, it had been "so altered, broken, and neglected, by planting in uncertain stories and legends, with a multitude of responds, verses, vain repetitions, commemorations, and synodals,"† as to have become wholly unintelligible. The reading of two Lessons in every service, one from each Testament, and in the order of the canon, is in accordance with primitive and Presbyterian usage; serves to mark the development and unity of divine revelation under both dispensations; and instructs both minister and people in the knowledge of God. But we may doubt whether a daily course of Lessons, as of Psalms,

---

others, engaged in preparing the Geneva Bible. See Horne's Biblical Bibliography, pp. 70—75.

* Westminster Directory: Reading of the Scriptures.

† King Edward's Prayer-book, Preface concerning the Service of the Church.

is not less suited to modern habits of public worship than a yearly course for Sundays alone; and have therefore added such a Table, which has the high sanction of the Church of Scotland.*

As to the *Proper Lessons* and *Proper Psalms*, or such as are severally proper to the different Sundays of the church year, we only remark, in passing, that they apparently befit the Lord's Day Service better than the Daily Prayer, which latter office is adjusted to the civil rather than to the ecclesiastical calendar, and would seem to require a rehearsal of the sacred books in their inspired connection and canonical order, as fundamental and preliminary to the more dogmatic re-arrangement of them in the Sunday service.

The *Apocryphal Scriptures* are omitted not merely because of their spurious claim and erroneous contents, but also because their use in the form of Lessons cannot but adulterate "the very pure Word of God."† And on the same principle, the discarded Lessons from the Book of the *Apocalypse* are restored.

It was a primitive custom, and is also directed in the Book of Common Order,‡ that the reading of the Scriptures should be intermingled with the singing of Psalms; and the *Canticles*, which are the fixed portions of the office, serve this purpose of relieving the attention after the Lessons, and giving life and variety to the service.

The *Te Deum Laudamus*, called in the Breviary the "Canticle of Ambrose and Augustine," from an old legend that at their baptism it was sung alternately by them as composed by inspiration, is one of the earliest Christian hymns of praise, and has also somewhat "the appearance of a choral paraphrase of the Creed." The reading and musical pointing of the English edition are retained without alteration.§

---

* Aids to Devotion, prepared by a Com. of Gen. Assemb.
† Preface of 1549. It was also proposed in 1689, "that the *Apocryphal Lessons* and those of the Old Testament which are too *Natural*, be thrown out." Calamy, p. 453. See Conf. of Faith, chap i
‡ Book of Pub. Pr., Appendix 350.
§ A verbal improvement was proposed in 1689. "That those words in the *Te Deum*, 'Thine Honourable, true, and Only Son,' be turned

The *Benedicite,* or "Song of the Three Children," was added after the Te Deum for alternative use, during Lent or at discretion; but its apocryphal character made it less acceptable to the Presbyterians than "some Psalm or Scripture hymn;" and the *Laudate Dominum,* (Ps. 148,) of which it is a lyrical exposition, has been substituted for it, as further recommended at the semi-Presbyterian revision in 1689.*

The *Benedictus,* (Luke i. 68,) or "Song of the Prophet Zacharias," was one of the first New Testament hymns, and has been used from a remote period in the position where it occurs, after the Lessons, as expressing praise for the fulfilment of the Old in the New dispensation.

The *Jubilate Deo,* (Ps. 100), a Psalm of Thanksgiving, was added as an alternate to the Benedictus, when that song should have been read immediately before in the daily course of Lessons.

The corresponding Canticles† at Evening Prayer, *Magnificat,* (Luke i. 46,) or "Song of the Virgin Mary," *Nunc Dimittis,* (Luke ii. 29,) or "Song of Simeon," with their alternate Psalms, *Cantate Domino,* (Ps. 98,) and *Benedic anima mea,* (Ps. 103,) follow the Prophecies and Epistles as appropriate hymns of praise for the blessings of a completed revelation, and were early used in the Calvinistic as well as primitive churches.‡

The *Apostles' Creed* seems naturally to ensue upon the Lessons as a personal confession of faith in the Scriptures, of which it is but a doctrinal summary, orthodox in its purport, catholic in its usage, and liturgical in its style. As it was not fully developed until the Second or Third Century, it could not have been compiled by the Apostles, according to the legend, which attributes a clause to each of them; though it appears to have originated in the baptismal formula with gradual accretions, and to have been at first the individual profession

---

into 'thine Only-begotten Son,' *Honourable* being only a civil term, and nowhere used in *Sacris.*" Calamy, p. 454.

* Exceptions; Appendix. Proctor, p. 147.

† It was proposed, in 1689, to substitute *Psalms* for the New Testament *Canticles.* Compare Calamy, p. 454, and Prot. Episc. Prayer book

‡ Eutaxia, p. 27.

of converts or catechumens, rather than an ordinary act of public worship.* It was retained in all the Protestant Confessions, is the text and frame-work of Calvin's "Institutes of Theology," and not only lies at the basis of our own Catechisms, but is given as a formula to be taught to children as part of their training for the Lord's Supper.†

As in the beginning of the service the minister declares the divine grace after the people have confessed their sins, so here at length, after the minister has declared the divine word, the people confess their faith, and are thus in readiness for those more mature devotions, the supplications, intercessions, and thanksgivings which are to follow.

From this point, according to the Prayer-book in the hands of the Savoy Commissioners, the office was thus continued:

Minister. The Lord be with you,
Answer. And with thy Spirit.
Minister. Let us pray.

Lord have mercy upon us.
Christ have mercy upon us.
Lord have mercy upon us.

¶ *Then the Minister, Clerks, and people shall say the Lord's prayer in English with a loud voice.*

Our Father, which art in heaven, &c.

¶ *Then the Minister standing up shall say,*

O Lord, show thy mercy upon us.

Answer. And grant us thy salvation.
Minister. O Lord, save the King.
Answer. And mercifully hear us when we call upon thee.
Minister. Endue thy ministers with righteousness.
Answer. And make thy chosen people joyful.
Minister. O Lord, save thy people.
Answer. And bless thine inheritance.
Minister. Give peace in our time, O Lord.
Answer. Because there is none other that fighteth for us, but only thou, O God.
Minister. O God, make clean our hearts within us.
Answer. And take not thy Holy Spirit from us.

---

* The *Nicene Creed* seems to have been reserved in all the Reformed Churches for the Communion as the proper Eucharistical Confession of Faith; the Apostles' Creed being, strictly speaking, a Baptismal Confession. See Dr. Krauth's Sunday Service, pp. 46, 47. Proctor, p. 228. Bunsen's Hippolytus, vol. ii. p. 92.

† Directory, chap. ix.

THE REVISED DAILY SERVICES. 97

For the reasons already mentioned,* we have not felt at liberty to retain more of this portion than the connection seems to require. The Lesser Litany, the repetition of the Lord's Prayer and the versicular petitions for the King, for Ministers, for the People, and for Peace, however beautiful they may be considered in a liturgical light, are suited only to a choral service, and as to their import superseded by the more Protestant forms of prayer which conclude the office. But the mutual *Salutation* of minister and people, which was a primitive, if not apostolic formula, is appropriate to the parties before entering the divine presence as suppliants; and the first and last couplet of versicles, which are respectively taken from the 85th and 51st Psalms, recommend themselves as suitable introductory petitions with which to begin the prayers following.

The *Collect for the Day* here enters as a link of the church-year connecting the Daily with the Sunday service, and when the Proper Lessons have been read before it, it may be relevant; but it is better reserved for the office in which it originated, and where alone, in most cases, its fitness can become fully apparent.

The *Collect for Peace*, which is not in the ancient Daily office, belongs to a special service in the Sacramentary, and is of the nature of an occasional prayer,† suitable to a warlike age, and perhaps to the troubled state of public affairs at the time the Prayer-book was formed.‡ It is certainly a beautiful petition, and has acquired new meaning and force from the present distracted state of our country; but that it should have been recited at other times, and for generations, without regard to its irrelevancy, only shows how impossible it is to frame a liturgy on the principle of an enforced uniformity, and may illustrate the general criticism passed

---

* See page 91 above, and also the Episcopalian proposals for the comprehension of the Presbyterians. "To omit all the responsal Prayers to the Litany." Calamy. p. 320.

† It appears in the *Missa pro Pace*, placed after the *Missa tempore belli*, and also among the Litany Collects; and although found in the Sunday service, yet it was not used in the week day or ferial offices. Compare Miss. Rom., Brev. Rom., and Proctor's **Comparative Table p. 448.** ‡ Procter, p. 238.

G

by the Presbyterians upon the Collects, that some of them have "no suitableness with the occasions upon which they are used, but seem to have fallen in rather casually, than from an orderly contrivance."*

The two *Collects for Grace*, the one at Morning and the other at Evening Prayer, are of very ancient origin, and the only collects obviously pertinent to a Daily office. The first phrase of the latter, "Lighten our darkness, we beseech thee, O Lord," is especially suitable to a twilight service; but to use the former, with its expression, "the beginning of this day," so late as noon or mid-day, is a solecism which, together with that involved in the invariable use of the other collects, may be obviated by attention to the preceding rubric concerning the use of the Litany.

(III.) We next enter upon our third and last division, beginning at the point where the old Latin, and the early English office ended. The remaining Prayers are mainly a Puritan accretion of forms which grew out of the felt unsuitableness of the preceding Versicles, and Collects, to Protestant worship in a popular assembly, and are framed upon the principle enunciated by the Presbyterians in 1661; "the Holy Scriptures, both of the Old and New Testament, intimating the people's part in public prayer to be only with silence and reverence to attend thereunto, and to declare their consent in the close by saying *Amen.*"†

The *Prayer for the Chief Magistrate and all in Authority* is the English "Prayer for the King's Majesty," adapted to American ideas of government by substituting for the words, "the only Ruler of princes," the more republican and equally scriptural phrase, "the Blessed and Only Potentate," and by inserting less personal petitions in place of the loyal request, "grant him in health and wealth *long to live*," which is very becoming under a monarchy, but not so suitable to a ruler whose political existence terminates every four years.‡ The whole prayer is in accordance with apostolic injunc-

---

* Exception XVI. † Exception III. See Appendix.
‡ Compare the alterations here made with analogous phrases in the Collect for the King; Communion Office; English Prayer-book.

tion and with universal feeling, is scriptural in style and purport, and no doubt originated at a very early period of the Reformation, though it does not appear in King Edward's First Prayer-book, and was used as the first of the occasional prayers at the close of the Litany until 1661, when it was transferred to its present position.

The *Prayer for Ministers and Congregations* is the ancient Collect, as amended by the Parliamentary Committee in 1641, and the Royal Commission of 1689,* and more exactly conformed to the doctrine of ministerial parity and communion. The title of Bishop, though scriptural and Presbyterian,† is not yet so generally attributed to ministers as to admit of its use in a form of devotion without misapprehension.

The *Prayer for all Conditions of Men*, or General Intercession, by whomsoever composed, originated in the Presbyterian revision as a substitute for the Collects, and is evidently modelled upon, if not largely quoted from, Calvinistic prayers, already authorized and domesticated in England.‡ The word "finally" seems inappropriate in so short a form, and is supposed to indicate that originally it was much longer, including such petitions for the king, clergy, and people, as are found in the preceding Versicles and Collects. But when the latter were retained by the Episcopalians at the last revision, it became necessary to omit the former, somewhat at the expense of the connection. The break might possibly be supplied by restoring, from the sources whence the form was taken, some addition of this kind: "And we also beseech thee, be merciful to all Christian States and Rulers, that under them thy true religion may be everywhere maintained, manners reformed, and sin punished, according to the rule of thy

---

* Procter, p. 99. Calamy says it was proposed in 1689 that "those words in the Prayer for the Clergy, *who alone workest great marvels*, as subject to be ill interpreted by persons vainly disposed, shall be thus. Who alone art the Author of all good gifts." Life of Baxter, p. 454.

† Conf. of Faith, chap. iv.

‡ Compare Exception XVI; Procter. p. 262; Liturgical Services, Queen Eliz., p. 266; Eutaxia, pp. 38, 39, 157.

Word." Such an amendment, besides being in keeping with the philanthropic spirit of the prayer, would complete the sense without interfering with that of the more particular intercessions preceding it.

The *General Thanksgiving* was composed by Reynolds, one of the Presbyterian Commissioners, and in accordance with their suggestion, to meet a defect which had been felt from the time of the Hampton Conference.* It breathes a thoroughly evangelical spirit, and in style is distinguishable from mediæval expressions of gratitude, which were in the form of Canticles and short Collects. The English edition has it among the "Occasional Prayers, to be used before the two final Prayers of the Litany, or of Morning and Evening Prayer;" but as here placed, for habitual use, it follows any Special Thanksgivings which have preceded it, as the General Intercession follows the Special Intercessions, and also forms a fitting climax to the whole office, which, having begun in a General Confession, may fittingly end with a General Thanksgiving.

The *Prayer of St. Chrysostom*, though not certainly traceable to that Saint, is of Greek origin, and appears in all ancient liturgies. As a concluding petition, founded upon the promise of divine grace and presence in all common or social prayers, it naturally arises in every heart in view of the petitions before offered.

The *Apostolic Benediction*, or benedictory prayer, does not appear in the Latin or early English office, was first placed at the end of Queen Elizabeth's Litany, and was not added to the Daily Prayer until the last revision. It was however customary in the primitive Church as a substitute for the ancient Levitical blessing, and doubtless grew out of the Apostolic valediction, used not only at the close of the Epistles, but also in dismissing worshipping assemblies, for which purpose it should be reserved, according to Presbyterian usage,† when

---

* Compare Exception XVII. ?2; Rejoinder, p. 267; Procter, p. 263, and authorities there quoted.

† It was also used in the Calvinistic Churches as a *Salutation*, in the form in which it occurs at the beginning of the Apostolic Epistles; the Minister pronouncing it as the first act of Divine Service; and it is still so used in the Reformed Dutch Church in this country. We

other services are to follow. Its use in the form here presented (with the pronoun *you* changed to *us*) as a common prayer, rather than as an official blessing, though not in strict accordance with the Scripture formula, may relieve any scruples which are felt when the conductor of the service is not an ordained minister.

If now the reader, in the light of these investigations, will compare the Daily Service in this Book with that in King Edward's First Book, he will be able to test the claims we have asserted. He will find that the two have scarcely anything in common, but such scriptural and ancient forms, as originated beyond the pale, and before the existence of the Church of England. So distinguishable indeed are all late editions by reason of their *Calvinistic*, *Puritan*, and *Presbyterian* accretions, that we do not hesitate to admit, that for all the purposes of rhetorical impression and artistic effect, they are far inferior to the beautiful service as it was first translated, and before the hand of innovation had marred its symmetry.* And if we prefer the former, it is only because we doubt if there can now be any safe or consistent mean between a liturgy that shall be primitive and Protestant, and one that is essentially mediæval and monastic.

SECT. V. *The Revised Litany.*

The Litany, which appears as a distinct office in all Prayer-books, was the earliest English, and probably

---

have placed it among the Introductory Sentences, where it may serve the same purpose. Either there or at the close of the service, as a form of greeting, or of dismissing the people, it fulfils its original design; but its occurrence in the midst of the service, as an ordinary prayer, is due to a want of such discretionary power in combining this office with others, as is suggested by the preceding rubric. Compare Conf. of Faith, pp. 441, 447, 503. And Princeton Review, April 1851. Article v. The Apostolic Benediction. Assembly's Digest, p. 83. Levitical Blessing. Num. vi. 22—26.

* " In approaching these Calvinistic innovations, our ritualist is sadly at fault. Loath to refer them to their unmistakeable sources, he takes a new journey into the past, and overhauls his accumulated stores of missals, pontificals, and sacramentaries, but comes back with nothing that ingenuity can twist into a semblance of paternity. We shrink from the cruelty of informing him at last, that these forms are the offspring of a system, which however venerated by his fathers, is identified to his mind with 'heresy, false doctrine, and schism,' from which he piously prays, 'Deliver us.'" Eutaxia, page 193.

also the earliest Roman and Greek form of public supplication. Its peculiar structure is said to have originated in a primitive custom of "bidding prayers;" the minister naming the subject of the petition, and the people ejaculating, *Lord, have mercy upon us*, or some like phrase. In process of time this usage, is supposed to have become a methodical form, in which the petitions and responses were always the same: and at length it reached liturgical perfection as chaunted in solemn processions of the clergy and people during the church fasts, or on occasions of public calamity.

The Litany, which was before the Savoy Commissioners for revision, had derived its framework and body from the old Latin form, but was also indebted for particular ideas and phrases to Hermann's Consultation or Reformation Book, as well as to the emendations of the English Reformers. The relative amount and value of these several portions will appear from the following version,* in which the parts due to Bucer are in italics, and those due to Cranmer in parentheses.

O God the Father, of heaven, have mercy upon us (miserable sinners.)

O God the Son, Redeemer of the world, have mercy upon us (miserable sinners.)

O God the Holy Ghost, (proceeding from the Father and the Son,) have mercy upon us (miserable sinners.)

O holy, blessed, and glorious Trinity, (three Persons and) one God, have mercy upon us (miserable sinners.)

Remember not, Lord, our offences, nor the offences of our forefathers; neither take thou vengeance of our sins: spare us (good) Lord, spare thy people, whom thou hast redeemed with thy most precious blood, and be not angry with us for ever,

Spare us, (good) Lord.

From all evil, (and mischief;) from sin, from the crafts and assaults) of the devil; from thy wrath, (and from everlasting damnation,)

(Good) Lord, deliver us.

---

* Compare the Litany of the Anglo-Saxon Church, (Procter, p. 251,) the Litany prepared by Bucer for Hermann's Consultation, (Baird's Book of Public Prayer, p. 67, 35,) the Roman Litanies, (Miss. Rom. and Brev. Rom.,) and the Litany in Queen Elizabeth's Prayer-book. Several subjects and expressions not found in the Anglo-Saxon Litany are common to both the Roman and the German Litanies, from whence they passed into Cranmer's English version with slight alterations.

THE REVISED LITANY.

(From all blindness of heart): from pride, (vain-glory, and hypocrisy,) from (envy), hatred, and malice, and all uncharitableness,

(Good) Lord, deliver us.

From fornication, and all other deadly sin; (and from all the deceits of the world, the flesh, and the devil.)

From lightning and tempest; from plague, pestilence, and famine; from battle and murder, and from sudden death.

(From all sedition, privy conspiracy, and rebellion; from all false doctrine, heresy, and schism; from hardness of heart, and contempt of thy Word and Commandment.)

By the mystery of thy holy Incarnation; by thy holy Nativity (and Circumcision) by thy Baptism, Fasting, and Temptation;

By thine Agony and bloody Sweat; by thy Cross and Passion; by thy precious Death and Burial; by thy glorious Resurrection and Ascension; and by the coming of the Holy Ghost;

In all time of our tribulation; in all time of our prosperity; in the hour of death, and in the day of judgment;

We sinners do beseech thee to hear us, (O Lord God;) and that it may please thee to rule and govern thy holy Church universal (in the right way.)

We beseech thee to hear us, (good Lord.)

(That it may please thee to illuminate all bishops, pastors, and ministers of the Church, with true knowledge and understanding of thy Word, and that both by their preaching and living they may set it forth, and show it accordingly;)

That it may please thee to bless and keep all thy people;

That it may please thee to give to all nations unity, peace, and concord;

That it may please thee (to give us an heart to love and dread thee, and diligently to live after thy commandments;)

That it may please thee to give to all thy people increase of grace, to hear meekly thy Word, and to receive it with pure affection, and to bring forth the fruits of the Spirit;

That it may please thee to bring into the way of truth, all such as have erred, and are deceived;

That it may please thee to strengthen such as do stand; and to comfort and help the weak-hearted; and to raise up them that fall; and finally to beat down Satan under our feet;

That it may please thee to succor, help, and comfort, all that are in danger, necessity, and tribulation;

That it may please thee to preserve (all that travel by land or by water,) all women laboring of child, all sick persons, and young children; and to show thy pity upon all prisoners and captives;

That it may please thee to defend, and provide for, the fatherless children and widows, and all that are desolate and oppressed;)

That it may please thee to have mercy upon all men;

That it may please thee to forgive our enemies, persecutors, and slanderers, and to turn their hearts;

That it may please thee to give and preserve to our use the kindly fruits of the earth, (so that in due time we may enjoy them;)

That it may please thee to give us true repentance; (to forgive us all our sins, negligences, and ignorances; and to endue us with the grace of thy Holy Spirit to amend our lives according to thy Holy Word;)

Son of God, we beseech thee to hear us.
O Lamb of God, who takest away the sins of the world, grant us thy peace;
O Lamb of God, who takest away the sins of the world, have mercy upon us.

The result of this comparison will show that while the general model of the ancient litanies has been preserved, yet the contents have been materially enlarged and modified in each of its particular divisions.

The *Invocations*, which form the introductory portion, and in the old offices were a long series of addresses to the Virgin, to angels and archangels, patriarchs, apostles, martyrs, and confessors, became at the Reformation restricted to the Three Sacred Persons of the Trinity; but their responsive repetition is peculiar to the English Litany, as also certain added phrases which seem to ensure orthodoxy somewhat at the expense of fitness.

The *Deprecations*, or petitions for deliverance from the various sins, evils, and calamities to which mankind are subject, are the ancient series, prefaced with a prayer or anthem which occurs in the Breviary between the Penitential Psalms and the Litany, and enlarged by several Protestant additions. An unprejudiced critic might question whether the epithet "*good Lord*," interpolated by Cranmer, is any improvement upon the original, (*Libera nos Domine*.) But on the other hand, it may be doubted whether the proposal of the Presbyterians to change the words "sudden death" to "dying suddenly and unprepared," although in accordance with the original, (a subitanea et improvisa morte,)* is not a scruple sufficiently met by the connection in which the phrase occurs, and hardly worth the risk of innovation.

The *Obsecrations*, or pleadings for mercy, are a recital of the grounds on which the previous deprecations are made, or the argument of the suppliant from the merits of Christ as illustrated in his whole earthly work and mission. They form the most solemn portion of the service, and carry in them a tone of all but inspired

---

* See Exceptions, Hermann's Litany, and Brev. Rom. Litaniæ.

pathos and fervor, suited at once to incite and express the deepest emotions of awe, penitence, and love.

The *Intercessions*, which then follow as a still higher act of supplication, are the largest, and by far the most Protestant portion of the office. Beginning with a petition for the Church universal, they comprise, in a natural order, the different classes and conditions, both civil and ecclesiastical, for whom public prayer should be offered, together with such special mercies and graces as are suited to all the common vicissitudes of human experience. It would be difficult to imagine any topic of ordinary intercession which is not found in this beautiful summary, and perhaps impossible to improve the arrangement. The only changes made are such as seem required by our simpler forms of polity; the substitution of "Rulers and Magistrates" for "King, Princess, Nobles, and Parliament," and of "Pastors and Ministers" for "Bishops, Pastors, and Ministers," which latter phrase of Cranmer was altered at the last revision to "Bishops, Priests, and Deacons," "an expression," says Proctor, "more distinctly opposed to Presbyterian notions of the Christian ministry." The corresponding suffrage in Hermann's Litany, was, "That it may please thee to preserve in soundness of Word and holiness of life, all Pastors and Ministers of thy Church."* We have also added from the same source, a petition for the unity of the church and increase of the ministry, which seems to be especially required by the present state of Christendom and heathendom.

After the Intercessions, in the Latin office, came the *Agnus Dei*, forming in the English service a fit conclusion; and as what follows does not seem suited to popular worship, at least on ordinary occasions, the Rubric suggests discretion in using it, which is also in accordance with one of the "Proposals" to the Presbyterians in 1668.†

The *Lesser Litany*, as the threefold or ninefold invocations of Christ are called, is the early Greek form,

---

* Compare Hermann's Litany and Liturgy of Evan. Lutheran Church, 1855.
† Calamy, vol. 1, p. 330, and Pres. Epis. Prayer book.

and was probably the germ of the Greater Litany, which afterwards grew up in the Roman Church. It was chaunted responsively in the ancient processions, at the beginning, as well as at the end of the Litaneutical Service, in connection with Psalmody, and with pauses for the Lord's Prayer and the Collects. As here inserted, and as viewed apart from the ceremonial in which it originated,* it is difficult to see its relevancy, or fitness for Protestant worship. This whole added portion, indeed, though containing separate versicles of great beauty, is confused and fragmentary, owing to the manner in which it was compiled by Cranmer from different parts of the ancient services. The first couplet and collect were taken from Bucer's Litany;† what follows to the end of the Gloria Patri, from the choral introduction to a Rogation Service; and then are inserted certain Versicles designed to be used in time of War (*in tempore belli.*)‡ Perhaps this latter section may serve to distinguish the discretionary, from the ordinary part of the Litany, as a supplement suitable only to occasions of public calamity.

Besides the concluding Prayer of St. Chrysostom, a series of *Occasional Prayers and Thanksgivings* have accumulated since the reign of Elizabeth, which, at the last revision, were placed under a separate heading, and in this edition will be found among the Additional Services, noticed in our last section.

This Litany might be appropriately used either as a distinct office, according to its original structure, with a selected psalm, lesson, and hymn, or in combination with the Daily or Sunday Service, as suggested in the different rubrics pertaining to these several offices.

Sect. VI. *The Revised Sunday Service.*

Under both dispensations, the seven-fold division of time, founded in natural as well as divine law, has generally prevailed for purposes alike of rest and of devotion, with the difference only that the Christian Sabbath falls upon the first day of the week instead of

---

* See Miss. Rom. Litaniæ.   † Book of Public Prayer, p. 70.
‡ Proctor, p. 257.

the last. It was called the *Lord's day*, after the example of St. John, and perhaps in allusion to our Saviour's resurrection upon that day of the week; and it is still so called in all ancient liturgies, the English Prayerbook having in this respect departed from scriptural and catholic usage.* Other things being equal, the Dominical or Christian title is certainly preferable, at least in a book of devotion, to the pagan name *Sunday*,† or even to the Jewish name *Sabbath;* and if we have not in all cases adopted this suggestion of the Presbyterian Revisers,‡ it is only because the introduction of such a phrase as *the Lord's day* throughout the calendar would now lead to much vague and inelegant circumlocution; and a narrow usage and false taste have combined to make it impracticable.

It seems to have been the primitive custom to celebrate the Lord's Supper in connection with the Lord's day, as a weekly communion, and the proper culmination of every Christian service; and all the ancient liturgies are constructed upon this theory. But inasmuch as modern habits of worship have rendered the practice obsolete, and its presumed continuance equivocal,§ and since, moreover, the so-called Ante-Communion is already practically dissevered from the Communion itself by the interposition of collects, lessons, and sermons incongruous with it, we have placed the anterior portion of the office where alone it occurs and belongs, after the Daily Service and before the Proper Services with which it is immediately connected. This simpler and more consecutive arrange-

---

* In the Latin offices, Saturdays are called Sabbaths. (Sabbata;) Sunday, the Lord's day. (Dominica;) and the Sundays after Trinity are reckoned as the Lord's days after Pentecost, (Dominica post Pentecosten)—a phraseology which certainly has the merit of being scriptural.

† "The retention of the old Pagan name of '*Dies Solis*,' or 'Sunday,' for the weekly Christian Festival, is, in great measure, owing to the union of Pagan and Christian sentiment with which the first day of the week was recommended by Constantine to his subjects, Pagan and Christian alike, as the 'venerable day of the Sun.'" Stanley's Hist. of Eastern Church, p. 291.

‡ Exception XI.

§ Compare Presbyterian Exception, Episcopalian **Answer**, **and Presbyterian Rejoinder**. Documents, pp. 116, 264, 255.

ment may diminish still more that inconvenience of which the Reformers complained in the ancient offices, when "the manifold changings of the service was the cause, that to turn the book only was so hard and intricate a matter, that many times there was more business to find out what should be read, than to read it when it was found out,"* and at the same time secure the liberty of using the services separately or in combination, as taste, prejudice, or custom will dictate.

The whole Sunday Office may, therefore, be considered in three general divisions: 1. The Order for Divine Service on the Lord's Day, or the ordinary and fixed portions, consisting of the introductory Collect, the Lord's Prayer, Commandments, Beatitudes, and Creed. 2. The Proper Services, or variable portions, consisting of the Collects, Epistles, and Gospels proper to the different Sundays of the Church-year. 3. The Communion Service, or Holy Supper to be added to the ordinary service as often as parochial authority will appoint.† We shall find, as we proceed, that of these several parts, the first and third are traceable to primitive and Presbyterian sources, while the second has derived its present form from a Presbyterian revision.

The first division of the office, what we have termed the *Order for Divine Service on the Lord's Day*, corresponds in its structure and purport to the service of Catechumens or Hearers of the Word, preliminary to the Eucharist in the primitive Church, and also substantially agrees with the "Order of Worship," now customary in our churches, its fixed portions serving as examples or summaries of the several parts of our ordinary service. It is essentially a homiletical office, properly culminating in a sermon, and is not necessarily connected either with the Festival services or with the Communion, as it existed long before the church-year was matured, and was originally detached from

---

* Preface to King Edward's First Prayer-book.

† An undesigned correspondence may be discerned between those several divisions and the *Ordo, Proprium*, and *Canon* of the ancient service; but all the details of the arrangement proceed upon totally different principles.

the Lord's Supper, the catechumens or hearers being dismissed as soon as the Sacrament began.* It is, in fact, the most scriptural, apostolic, catholic, and Presbyterian form which the book contains.

The *Lœtatus Sum*, (Ps. 122,) placed before the office, was one of the fifteen "Songs of Degrees" sung while ascending the steps of the ancient temple to engage in the public service. It is given as an example of an introductory chant, corresponding to the *Introit* in the Latin office, or to the selected *Metrical Psalm* in the modern office. It might take the place of the choir *Voluntary*, becoming so customary in our churches. The English usage was derived from Geneva, though at first it seems to have been a crude addition to the established service rather than an integral part of it.† Were the prose psalmody substituted for the metrical, and the chant selected always of an *introductory* tenor, a prelude suited to compose the mind according to the nature of the occasion, the fitness and advantage of this initial act of praise would become much more obvious.

The *Collect for Purity*, with which the office properly begins, was one of the preparatory prayers used in the ancient service, and corresponds in position and import to the introductory petition or "Invocation" prescribed by the Directory.‡ Such a solemn appeal to the great Searcher of hearts for grace and aid, on entering his presence and engaging in his service, will be the spontaneous impulse of every true worshipper.

The *Lord's Prayer*, which immediately follows, is placed after rather than before the preparatory petition, in accordance with the most catholic as well as Presbyterian usage, and also because it is then more likely to be used by the congregation "with understanding, faith, reverence, and other graces necessary to the right performance of the duty of prayer."§

The *Commandments* are not found in King Edward's

---

* See Bunsen's Hippolytus and his Age, vol. ii. The Church and House-book of the Ancient Christians, pp. 47, 48. Neander's Church History, vol. i. pp. 305, 327, 323.
† Proctor, pp. 59, 175; Eutaxia. p. 126.
‡ Chap. v.   § Larger Catechism, Q. 187.

First Book, which, at this point, in common with the old office, has the Lesser Litany, or *Kyrie eleison*, to be said or sung nine times:

   iii. Lord, have mercy upon us.
   iii. Christ, have mercy upon us.
   iii. Lord, have mercy upon us.

At the Calvinistic revision, these responses seem to have been retained, but with the insertion of a commandment before each of them, and the addition to each of the further petition, "and incline our hearts to keep this law," and also of the summary prayer at the close, "and write all these laws in our hearts, we beseech thee." Such a use of the Decalogue in public worship, though common to all the Presbyterian liturgies, had been hitherto unknown in the mediæval offices with which it is plainly out of keeping, and it is known to have been borrowed from the Lord's Day Service of Pollanus, from which also was taken the concluding petition.* The same feeling which prompted the penitential introduction to the Daily Prayer would seem also to have suggested this addition, and its fitness, especially when the Communion is to follow, must be obvious. The approved translation has been used in compliance with the Presbyterian Exceptions; and although, for the same reason, the kneeling posture and audible responses are not enjoined or even suggested, yet it may be doubted whether one should listen to the Reading of the Law as to any ordinary lesson of Scripture, or if its due effect, as the instrument of conviction, is not to bring both mind and body into a lowly attitude.

After the commandments, in the English edition, came two Collects for the King, in place of which the American Episcopalian edition has, very appropriately, our Lord's *Summary of the Law and the Prophets*, together with a suitable Collect—an idea which was also suggested by the Presbyterian revisers, and had already been illustrated in the liturgy of Pollanus.† Such an epitome of

---

* Compare King Edward's First and Second Prayer-books and Pollanus' Liturgia Peregrinorum.

† The Collect is the second at the end of the Communion. The following is the Petition in Pollanus' Liturgy: "Domine Deus,

the Old Testament, in the words of its Divine Expounder, serves to mark the transition to the New Testament, and to carry forward the worshipper from the humbling discipline of the law into the light and liberty of the gospel.

The *Collect*, *Epistle*, and *Gospel* are the more gladsome devotions which then follow, breathing the Christian in distinction from the Hebrew spirit. As set forth in the ancient offices, they are a series of carefully arranged services, epitomizing throughout the year the whole New Testament history and doctrine in the words of Christ and his apostles, together with appropriate petitions hallowed by immemorial usage, and are unquestionably suited to train up a far more intelligent type of devotion than that induced by the random use of Scripture which prevails in many churches. At the same time, it would be only falling into the other extreme to be so bound even to this beautiful system as to have no discretion when occasions or circumstances plainly require different selections.

The *Beatitudes*, which are found only in this edition, may serve as a summary of the Gospel, corresponding to the Commandments as a summary of the Law, the posture of penitents and disciples being now changed to that of thankful worshippers. They are in keeping with the ancient custom, at first retained by the Reformers, of standing at the reading of the Gospel with the joyful ascription, "Glory be to thee, O Lord;" and were recommended to be placed in this office by the Semi-Presbyterian Commission of 1689, as an occasional substitute for the Commandments with the response, "Lord, have mercy upon us, and make us partakers of this blessing." They also appear as a permanent Gospel Lesson in the Sunday Morning Prayer of King Edward's Primer.*
But whether used as an ordinary lesson, or as a series

Pater misericors, qui hoc decalogo per servum tuum Mosen nos Legis tuæ justitiam docuisti; dignare cordibus nostris eam ita tuo spiritu inscribere, ut nequicquam deinceps in vita magis optemus, aut velimus, quam tibi obedientia consumatissima placere in omnibus, per Jesum Christum filium tuum. Amen."
* Compare Procter, p. 151.

of solemn benedictions, they cannot fail to meet with a response in every Christian heart.

The *Gloria in Excelsis Deo*, which next follows, was transferred at the Calvinistic revision of King Edward's First Book from the beginning to the close of the office, and there placed as a post-communion doxology. It would, however, occur too seldom if confined to that position, and seems to follow naturally, in our arrangement, as an exalted act of praise for the blessings of the gospel already felt, or yet to be fully experienced by the beatified believer. The hymn itself is one of the earliest hymns of the Eastern Church, and is supposed to have been founded upon the angelic song at the birth of the Saviour. The spirit of that divine original seems indeed to linger in its sublime words, lifting the soul beyond the sins and sorrows of life, and bearing it away into a region of heavenly purity and peace.

The *Nicene Creed*, also a product of the Eastern Church, may appropriately take the place of the Apostles' Creed on communion-days, as being that more precise and full confession of faith proper to a service in which the "hearer" is supposed to have become a "believer," and the catechumen trained into a communicant. Born in the great Council of Nicæa, as the fruit of the assembled wisdom of the Church, in an age when doctrinal truth was prized above every worldly interest, it remains among us to this day the most ancient, orthodox, and catholic symbol in Christendom, and may more perfectly realize the Communion of Saints on earth than any other uninspired words that could now be recited in a Christian assembly.

When Morning Prayer is offered immediately before and in connection with this office, the Creed will of course be omitted, and the Sermon will follow the Gloria in Excelsis, or such other hymn as may have been appointed by the minister. But otherwise, in order to render the service complete, the Litany will here be used, followed by the Hymn, Announcements, and Collection.

The *Collect before Sermon*, is taken from the ancient form customary at the reading of the Gospel, and expresses a petition which, whether offered privately by the preacher alone, or silently by preacher and hearer together, is always felt to be suitable to the parties at that juncture.

The *Sermon* itself has ever been the great central feature of primitive and Protestant worship, and still serves to distinguish the evangelizing from the mere ritualistic type of Christianity. The Directory, especially the Westminster edition, is careful to exalt this function of the Christian ministry, and insists upon a preacher "presupposed to be versed in the whole body of theology, but most of all in the Holy Scriptures, and to have skill in the original languages, and in such arts and sciences as are handmaids unto divinity." Viewed in a liturgical light the Sermon grows naturally out of the Epistle and Gospel, which may either suggest the theme,* or be themselves selected with reference to it, when the occasion is extraordinary, or the minister's taste and judgment shall dictate some different routine of topics.

The *Collect after Sermon* is an early English form composed by the reformers, and answers to a rule in the Directory as well as to a common feeling that prayer is needed not only for "the sound preaching and conscionable hearing of the Word," but also that we may become doers thereof. To further which ends more particular petitions "in relation to the subject treated of in the discourse" will be offered by every workman who rightly divides the Word of truth.†

The *Collects, Ascriptions, and Benedictions*, added for discretionary use, may serve as examples of different modes of ending the last prayer or of closing the whole service. They are taken from the Scriptures and from the Ancient liturgies, except the first Collect, which is due to the Proposals of 1689.‡

In using this Order of Service, it is obvious that much will depend upon the manner in which its variable portions are arranged from Sunday to Sunday; and to a consideration of this question our second general division is devoted.

---

* See above, chap. iv.   † Direct., chap. v.
‡ See Revised Collects in Book of Pub. Prayer. It appears also in the Institution Office. Prot. Episc. Prayer-book.

SECT. VII. *The Revised Proper Services.*

It is the doctrine of our standards that there is no day commanded to be kept holy under the Gospel, except the Lord's Day; but as it is not enjoined so neither is it forbidden to have a yearly course of Services for the observance and improvement of that day; nor can there be any sound objection to such an arrangement, but rather much to recommend it, if only it proceed upon some scriptural and rational principle, be not imposed upon the conscience, and be in accordance with the purest and most catholic usage. Besides the good accruing to the Church at large by thus promoting in a practical form the Communion of Saints there will be yielded in each congregation those two essentials of fresh devotion and effective preaching, an *occasion* for the hearer and a *theme* for the speaker, and the consequent means of celebrating the Lord's days throughout the year with greater profit and solemnity.

Now, it is undeniable that the elements of such a system originated in the Church of the Apostles and were retained in greater or less perfection by all the Reformed Churches, except the Church of Scotland during its later history and the Church of England during the time when the Presbyterian framers of our standards were in league with the Covenanters and Independents. As soon as they were released from that political compact they returned to a more scriptural stand point, and according to Apostolic teaching and example, would have allowed a voluntary observance of such Dominical or Christian festivals as breathe the spirit of the Lord's day, and are, in most cases, actually blended with it.*

On the other hand, however, it must also be granted that this primitive calendar, having originated in a rude age of the world, has grown up in defiance of all accu-

---

* Compare Neander's Hist. of Christian Rel. and Church, vol. i. p. 295; Schaff's History of the Apostolic Church, p. 557; Eutaxia, p. 28. Presbyterian Exceptions and Rejoinder, and the Epistle of St. Paul to the Romans, chap. xiv

It is to be observed that the *Appendix* to the Westminster Directory against Holy Days and Festivals was expunged from our edition at the revision by the General Assembly.

rate chronology and history, and for centuries has been steadily supplanted by the modern civil calendar, until now it remains only as a mass of ingenious anachronisms. And it may be questioned whether, in the New World, the sentimental advantage of keeping it in concert with the churches which adhere to it in the Old World, is to be weighed against its practical inconvenience and absurdity, when that nest of chronic puzzles which prefaces the Prayer-book could be reduced to a single Table, and the *principle* of the whole still retained, by so simple a change as that of fixing Easter for the first or second Sunday in April.*

Easter-day, which at first fell upon a week-day, until by a decree of the Council of Nicæa it was made to fall upon a Sunday, grew out of the Jewish year as a Christian Passover, in the same manner that the Lord's day grew out of the Jewish week as a Christian Sabbath, the one being an annual and the other a weekly observance of his resurrection. It forms the epoch from which the whole Christian year dates, the seasons before it being mainly devoted to a rehearsal of Christ's life and passion, and those following it, to a rehearsal of his example and doctrine.

Advent, *Epiphany* and *Lent*, are the seasons observed in approaching Easter from about the beginning of December until about the beginning of April, and the Lord's days during that period may commemorate his Incarnation, Nativity, Circumcision, Baptism, Temptation, Agony, Crucifixion, and Burial. *Ascension*, *Whitsunday* or *Pentecost* and *Trinity*, are the seasons observed in leaving Easter, from about the first of April until about the beginning of December, and the Lord's days during that period may commemorate his Resurrection, his Glorification with the Father, his Sending the Holy

---

* "There is one point in regard to the settlement of the Paschal question, which seems entirely to have escaped the Nicene Fathers, but which, probably, owing to their want of foresight, will, with each succeeding century, widen the divergence between civil and ecclesiastical usages. How many collisions and complications might have been avoided, had Easter been then, once for all, made a fixed, instead of a movable, festival!" Stanley's Eastern Church, p. 203.

Ghost, and all the peculiar lessons of the New Testament.

The devout recognition, with appropriate services, of the week-days commonly called *Christmas-day*, *Good-Friday*, and *Ascension-day*, is in accordance with Presbyterian and catholic usage; but the observation of Lent as a religious fast was objected to by the Presbyterians, "the example of Christ fasting forty days and nights being no more imitable nor intended for the imitation of a Christian, than any other of his miraculous works."

In compliance with the same authority the Proper Services appointed for *Saints' days* have been expunged, and the names of any Apostles and Evangelists left in the calendar are there simply for the preservation of their memories and other useful purposes.

The Proper Services which are retained are only such as appertain to the strictly Dominical festivals in honor of our Lord and in connection with his own Holy Day, and their addition to the ordinary service is left wholly discretionary. In the Latin Church they consisted of a number of intricate parts adjusted to the minute ritual which had overgrown the primitive order, such as the Introits, Graduals, Tracts, Gospels, Collects, Epistles, besides the Offertories, Secreta, Prefaces, Communions, and Post-communions connected with the celebration of the Lord's Supper. Of these none have been retained in the English Prayer-book but the Collects, Epistles and Gospels, which are really the most ancient portions, are in nowise inconsistent with the simple usages of Protestant worship, and owe the improved form in which they now appear to the Presbyterian revisionists.

The *Collect for the Day* is a brief petition collecting in a single sentence the devotional feeling proper to the festival to which it refers, or to the Gospel or Epistle with which it is connected. Many of the collects date from a very remote period, and are of great force and beauty as well in the original Latin as in the pure English in which they have come down to us. Some verbal errors in them were corrected at the instance of the Presbyterian Commissioners,* and a thorough revision of them was afterwards attempted by the Episcopalian Commissioners of 1689, on the principle of adapting them more closely to the Epistles and Gospels, and with the view of expressing more clearly the evangelical sentiment of their Presbyterian associates. As an attempt to remedy the vagueness and generality which mark a number of them, especially those for the Sundays after Trinity, the proposed amendments are praiseworthy; but in most cases they mar the ancient model without at the same time sufficiently gaining the object in view.

The *Epistle and Gospel for the Day* express in a more didactic form the sense of the collect, and are designed to inculcate the lessons proper to the occasion or festival to which they belong. They were rendered in the approved translation in accordance with the Presbyterian revision, and have been retained without alteration. Their antiquity and general fitness make them preferable to any new selections, and they are useful for devotional reading at other times.

Besides these ancient Proper services, the new features which have arisen in the modern office may be adapted to the church-year together with the sermon.

The *Introductory Psalm*, instead of being appointed at random, or as a mere general prelude, might be suited to the ecclesiastical season on the principle of the Introit retained in King Edward's First Prayer-book. Such a re-adjustment of the Psalter would serve to Christianize it, and to bring it more intelligently into divine worship; and if the whole Psalm were not in every instance relevant, the fit verses only might be used, or, what is better, Canticles formed out of different verses compiled from any of the poetical portions of the Scriptures. The *Table of Proper Psalms*, added as a help in making such selections, has been taken

---

* Compare the Presbyterian Exceptions to "the two Collects for St. John's day, and Innocent's, for the first day in Lent, for the fourth Sunday after Easter, for Trinity Sunday, for the sixth and twelfth Sunday after Trinity, for St. Luke's day, and Michælmas day," with the same in the English Prayer-book.

partly from the ancient offices and partly from various modern liturgies.*

An arrangement of *Hymns* on the same principle still further ensures unity and beauty to these commemmorative services.

Even a course of Sermons or *Homilies*, well selected from approved divines, and adapted to the lessons of the yearly course, though it would be too unwieldy to form part of a public liturgy, might be an advantage in the case of such worshippers as are deprived of a stated ministry.†

According to the theory already advocated, the Proper services are suitable to the Sunday, rather than to the Daily, office; but there may be seasons or circumstances in which both offices can be conveniently and profitably used; and the *Table of Proper Lessons to be read at Morning and Evening Prayer* will afford the means of substituting suitable selections in place of those of the Daily course.

Sect. VIII. *The Revised Communion Service.*

We next approach the most sacred portion of the office, or indeed of the whole book, and that for which the other services are but a preliminary training, leading to it as to the very crown and complement of all Christian worship, the "holy of holies" in the Church-service.

The *Lord's Supper* grew out of the Paschal Supper, with a change of symbols, the broken bread being used in place of the slain lamb to express and convey the benefits of Christ's sacrifice, and a Table substituted for the Altar, as the social feature of the rite. In the early Church it was unquestionably observed in the simplest manner as a spiritual service of Thanksgiving and Communion; but in process of time it became, in the Latin Church, the elaborate ritual called the Mass, and so continued until the Reformation, when the

---

* Compare King Edward's First Prayer-book, the Evangelical Lutheran Liturgy, and Liturgiæ Recusæ Exemplar.

† Confession of Faith, p. 452.

Protestant churches, with greater or less approximation, returned to the simplicity of the primitive institution.

The *Order for the Administration of the Lord's Supper or Holy Communion*, as amended by the Savoy Presbyterians, will be found, when historically traced and analyzed, substantially to contain: 1. The "Lord's Supper" of the Apostolical Church; 2. The "Eucharist" of the Primitive Church; 3. The earliest English Protestant "Order of Communion;"* 4. The Calvinistic "Form of Celebrating the Lord's Supper;" 5. The Westminster and American Directory for "Administration of the Lord's Supper." And it is believed that, as here presented, it retains every thing essential to either of these formularies, and nothing inconsistent with any of them.

The office may be conveniently considered in three parts: 1. The Ante-Communion, consisting of the Collection, the Prayer for the Church Militant, Exhortations, Words of Institution, Admonition and Invitation, Confession, Absolution, and Prayer of Humble Access; 2. The Communion, consisting of the Versicles, the Tersanctus, the Prayer of Consecration, the Ministration and Communion of the Bread and Wine; 3. The Post-Communion, consisting of the Thanksgiving, the Closing Hymn, and Benediction. We shall find that, while the first and last portions are essentially Protestant in their origin and structure, the intermediate portion retains all of the primitive and catholic service which is consistent with the Scriptures and with our own standards.

What we have termed the Ante-Communion portion is a series of preparatory and preliminary services through which the communicant passes, by natural

---

* This formulary, which was issued and in use some months in advance of the Prayer-book, was substantially taken by the English Reformers from the Reformed Service of Bucer and Melanctbon, and was also immediately translated and submitted by Coverdale to the examination of Calvin. who does not seem to have disapproved of it. It may be found in the "Liturgies of King Edward VI.; Parker Society." See also Coverdale's Letters to Calvin; Original Letters, First Series, p. 31.

advances of feeling, to the solemn acts of participation in the Communion itself. They are not found in the ancient office, but were affixed to it before it was translated and popularized, very much as the introductory portion of the Daily Prayer was prefixed to the ancient part of that office. As first used, indeed, they formed a distinct English Communion of the laity, ensuing upon the Latin Mass performed by the clergy, until the Prayer-book was compiled about a year afterwards, when they lost their provisional character, and became blended in a somewhat confused manner with certain translated portions of the old office.* They are here preserved, with but one or two additions, in the exact order in which they were first used, that they may serve the purpose to which they are so beautifully adapted, of inducing charity, penitence, assurance, and humility in the expecting communicant.

The *Rubrics*, introductory and concluding, are literally quoted from the Directory, and also those throughout the office, as far as practicable.

The *Exhortations* proceed upon the principle of the Apostolic Exhortation, "Let a man examine himself, and so let him eat of that bread and drink of that cup," and answer to the Preparatory Lecture prescribed by the Directory, and customary in Presbyterian churches. They might serve as samples upon which to model such addresses, or be used as stated forms according to the custom of some Calvinistic liturgies. The second Exhortation is attributed to Peter Martyr. The other two appear first in the "Order of Communion," but re-appear also in Knox's "Book of Common Order," and are thoroughly Calvinistic in tone and structure. They owe their present arrangement to the Presbyterian

---

* In the Prayer-book of 1549, the "Order of Communion" appears at the end of the old office unmutilated; but in 1552 it was prefixed to that office, with the exception of the 'Prayer of Humble Access," which was inserted between the Tersanctus and the Consecration Prayer. At the same time certain portions of the latter prayer were sundered from it, and placed apart at the very extremes of the office, where they form respectively the "Prayer for the Church Militant" and the "Post-Communion Thanksgiving." See the "Liturgies of King Edward," Parker Society; and also a comparative view in Chevalier Bunsen's Hippolytus, vol. ii. p. 173—204.

Exceptions, as also an added clause for the comfort of doubting Christians, taken from the Larger Catechism.

The *Collection for the Poor and other Pious Purposes*, placed next before the office, to be used in connection with it, or as a distinct act of worship, corresponds to the *Oblation* in the Eucharist, and to the *Offertory* in the Latin and English service. It seems at first to have consisted of contributions to the Agapæ or Love-Feast, or of gifts for the support of the ministry and the poor; but the multiplied objects of modern charity have disconnected it from the Sacrament which it might otherwise so fittingly precede, and rendered it scarcely more, sometimes less, than an ordinary part of divine service. For this reason, other Scripture sentences of various import have been added; and in compliance with the Presbyterian Exceptions the Apocryphal selections have been expunged.

The *Prayer for the Church Militant* is also not necessarily connected with the Communion, but may appropriately take the place of the ordinary prayer after sermon, and serve to extend the feeling of charity, expressed in the Collection, from the particular assembly of communicants to the whole Church universal into spiritual communion with which they are about to enter. Such a usage was common in the primitive Eucharist, and the form itself is very ancient, though in its structure and in certain expressions it resembles a prayer with the same title in Knox's Book of Common Order.

The *Words of Institution* are inserted in compliance with the Directory, and serve both as a warrant and a lesson to insure the intelligent reception of the Sacrament, especially when explained after the manner of the Exhortation following them. They form that portion of the rite which our Saviour himself dictated, and are afterwards repeated by the minister, while giving the elements, "in accordance with his example, institution, and command," as a declaration to the people, rather than as part of the consecrating prayer; the latter usage seeming to carry in it a notion of some transubstantiative effect upon the bread and wine to which the words refer.

The *Admonition* and *Invitation* have their warrant in the Apostolic Epistles and in the Directory, and owe their form to the "Order of Communion." They also correspond to the primitive usage of dismissing the catechumens and separating the communicants at the close of the ordinary service, with such exclamations as "No Profane!" "Let none depart entitled to stay!" and are designed at once to guard the Sacrament from an injurious effect upon "the profane, the ignorant, and the scandalous," and to encourage the timid, penitent, and believing in their advances.

The *Confession* is from the same source, somewhat abbreviated in form, and with an added clause from the Calvinistic Confession of Pollanus.* As a preliminary act in coming to the Communion, it is common to all liturgies, and dictated by universal Christian feeling. No language could be more deeply penitential, or more fittingly express the pungent convictions and fervid supplications with which the worthy communicant approaches the Sacrament.

The *Prayer for Absolution*, which then immediately follows, is a Protestant version of the old form, and suitably differs from that in the Daily service, by being precatory rather than declaratory in style. It is also appropriately followed by the more scriptural though less liturgical expression of the same sentiment, the *Comfortable Words*, proceeding on the Calvinistic principle of "raising sinners to the hopes of pardon" after confession, and also of reciting the revealed grounds upon which that pardon is sought, declared, and granted.

The *Prayer of Humble Access* is an entirely Protestant form, which was composed by the English Reformers for the "Order of Communion," and breathes the deeply religious spirit of the age in which it was produced. In the Prayer-book it became transferred to a later stage of the service, where it only breaks the continuity of feeling; but as first used, and here preserved in its original connection, it collects the feelings of mingled humility and assurance, resulting from the Confession and Absolution preceding it, and prepares the

---

* Proctor, p. 346.

suppliant for the more joyous devotions of the Eucharist then to follow.*

At this point we enter upon our second general division, which we have termed the Communion itself, and which is the most primitive and apostolic portion of the office, having been largely in use in the primitive Church, as well as in the modern Calvinistic liturgies.

The *Versicles* with which it begins, may mark the transition from the one portion to the other, with a befitting change of tone and posture, and also themselves appropriately herald the Thanksgiving. Especially the *Sursum Corda*† ("Lift up your hearts") was used in the early Christian assemblies as a warning to the worshipper to assume the devotional intention proper at this juncture; and the other responses, following between the minister and the communicant, may further serve to stir up and provoke an attentive mood and solemn expectancy as the critical part of the service approaches.

The *Preface*, which then introduces the acts of Thanksgiving and Praise, bears traces of the more liturgical style of a later age, when the free usages of primitive worship had begun to harden into a ritual. It varied, in the Latin office, with the recurring festivals of the Church year, and was designed to present the event or doctrine celebrated in each as the special ground of the following thanksgiving. Of these Proper Prefaces, only the five relating to the Nativity, Resurrection, and Ascension of Christ, the Mission of the Holy Ghost, and the Trinity, were retained in the English office. This is certainly, as far as it goes, an improvement. To celebrate the Lord's Supper in commemoration of an apostle, saint, or martyr, is a manifest perversion; but it is still doubtful whether even such an event as the Birth or Ascension of Christ is entirely congruous with a rite

---

* The last clause is amended in accordance with the Presbyterian Exceptions. Compare it also with "Order of Communion" and First and Second Prayer books of Edward VI. Parker Society edition.

† See Presbyterian Rejoinder, Documents, p. 210; "Apostolical Constitutions" in Bunsen's Hippolytus, vol. ii. p. 48; and Pollanus' Liturgia Peregrinorum.

expressly framed to symbolize his death and convey the benefits of his passion. Moreover, the interjection of such foreign ideas at this moment can only tend to interrupt the flow of devotion toward the Sacrament, and confuse the grateful feeling proper to it. We have therefore retained but a single Preface, setting forth the burden of the Eucharist itself, the great sacrifice of Christ upon the Cross, as the theme of exultant praise in receiving it. The language used for this purpose is taken from another portion of the office where it seems to occur less appropriately than in this connection.*

The *Tersanctus*, or *Trisagion*, so called from its threefold ascription of the word Holy, then follows in fulfilment of the Preface, as an exalted act of adoration and gratitude, lifting the worshipper into communion with the whole heavenly host, as if in anticipation of that glorious realization of the Eucharistic symbol, when the Lamb, appearing as it had been slain, becomes the centre of universal praise. This sublime hymn seems to have derived its theme from the seraphic vision in Isaiah, and has been in use in the Christian Church, as part of this service, from the most primitive times.†

The *Prayer of Consecration* is designed, in accordance with the Directory, to "set apart the elements from common use," by charging them with their appointed significance as emblems and pledges of that broken body and shed blood of Christ which they exhibit, by invoking the Holy Spirit to render them means of spiritual nourishment, and by imploring those inward graces necessary to their worthy reception. The language of the form is derived from very ancient sources, so amended by the English Reformers as to exclude all ideas of transubstantiation in the elements themselves, and with an added clause from the Westminster Catechism, expressing their effect in the believing recipient. The petition for the consecrating or blessing the ele-

---

* Compare Prefaces in Miss. Rom. and in English Prayer-book with this edition.
† See the Primitive Eucharist in Bunsen, p. 49.

ments, "with the Word and Holy Spirit," is taken from King Edward's Prayer-book, and is an addition suggested by the Presbyterians, and in accordance with the doctrine of our standards.*

The *Breaking of the Bread* is a ceremony which belonged to the rite as instituted by Christ and described by the apostles, which was common in the primitive and reformed liturgies, which is required by the Directory, and in accordance with the Presbyterian Exceptions, and which itself enters into the symbolical structure of the Sacrament by representing the breaking of Christ's body for us, and our communion with him and with one another as his members.†

The *Administration of the Elements* is prescribed according to the rules in the Directory, and is designed to be a devout repetition, as near as may be, of the original scene of the Lord's Supper; the Minister standing at a table rather than at an altar, and the communicants being assembled around or before it, while he gives them the sacred emblems in the name and with the words of Christ.‡

The *Sentences of Scripture* to be pronounced, during the distribution of each element, and the rubric explaining their use, are from the Calvinistic and Knoxian liturgies, and allowable according to the Directory, which prescribes no form of words for "putting the communicants in mind of the grace signified by the Sacrament." Such inspired declarations, aptly chosen,

---

* Confession of Faith, chap. xxix.; Larger Catechism, Q. 169, 170; Early Prayer-books and Presbyterian Exceptions.

† Hodge's Outlines of Theology. p. 505.

‡ In the Liturgy of Pollanus, the words used were, " Panis quem frangimus communicatio est corporis Christi; accipite, comedite memores corpus Christi pro vobis esse fractum. Calix benedictionis cui benedicimus communicatio est sanguinis Christi, qui pro vobis est fusus in remissionem peccatorum"—a form compiled from the different Scriptures relating to the Sacrament. The Westminster Directory has the following: "According to the holy institution, command, and example of our blessed Saviour Jesus Christ, I take this bread, and having given thanks, break it, and give it unto you. (There the minister, who is also himself to communicate, is to break the bread, and give it to the communicants:) *Take ye, eat ye; this is the body of Christ which is broken for you: do this in remembrance of him.*"

would seem to be preferable either to the repetition of the same formula to each communicant, or to the loose harangues to the whole assembly, which sometimes mar the service. It is a time when the simple Word of God will prove a better help to devotion than any words of man, uttered with rhetorical propriety, or in strained exhortation; and the practice has been found as acceptable as it is profitable.*

The *Silent Prayer*, after receiving the elements, is a primitive and catholic usage, would seem to be dictated by a spontaneous feeling, and has, besides, the incidental advantage of affording the minister as well as the communicant an interval for secret devotion.

The third and concluding portion of the office, termed the Post-Communion, is a brief series of services suited to incite and express the sentiments proper to the communicant on leaving the Lord's Table. Like the Ante-Communion or Preparatory Lecture, it is sometimes reserved as a separate service in the after part of the day, with a sermon or exhortation, designed to express the thankful feeling of the communicants, or to admonish them to walk worthy of their vocation as Christ's followers. As here arranged, it forms a fitting conclusion to the office, and is more in accordance with the Directory than a distinct service after the first glow of the sacramental devotion has faded.

The *Scripture Sentences after Communion* are taken in part from King Edward's Prayer-book, and may appropriately mark the transition to this portion of the office by expressing, according to the selection used, the feelings which will spontaneously arise at the moment.

The *Thanksgiving after Communion* is an act of devotion prescribed by the Directory, and common in all Presbyterian liturgies. The first of the two examples given formed the conclusion of the Consecration Prayer in 1549; but at the Calvinistic revision in 1552 it was transferred to its present position,* where alone it is

---

* Eutaxia, p. 56. Book of Public Prayer. Book of Common Order. Liturgies of German Reformed Church and Evangelical Lutheran Church.

* In the American Episcopal edition it is transferred back again to the Consecration Prayer, where it appears in connection with cer

fittingly offered, and where, moreover, it no longer implies a material oblation of the elements, but a spiritual oblation made by the communicants of their own persons, with praise and thanksgiving. In the language of St. Paul's exhortation to "present our bodies a living sacrifice, holy, acceptable to God, as our reasonable service." Such an act of grateful personal dedication of himself to Christ will be a spontaneous impulse of the communicant at this juncture, and could scarcely be expressed in more scriptural terms. The second example is also a strictly Protestant form, composed by the Calvinistic Reformers, and may serve to vary the feeling resulting from the Sacrament by expressing more the feeling of praise in connection with prayer for self-consecration. If the Lord's Prayer has not been used in the preceding service, it will be in accordance with liturgical law and usage to offer it also with the Thanksgiving.

The *Hymn* and *Doxology* will express, in still more joyous form, this thankfulness, and conclude the office as our Lord and his apostles concluded it, when they "sang an hymn and went out into the Mount of Olives." The "Gloria in Excelsis," or Greater Doxology, is prescribed in late editions; but the "Song of Simeon," "Lord, now lettest thou thy servant depart in peace," was in universal use at the close of the Calvinistic liturgy, and beautifully connects together ideas of the earthly and the heavenly Communion at the moment of dismissing the communicants. "They can rise no higher in this life. There is nothing beyond but heaven. Their longings find fit expression in the *Nunc Dimittis*."†

The *Blessing* follows in accordance with catholic usage. The form, compiled by Bucer, is here given in other editions, but in this is placed for ordinary use among the forms at the close of the Sunday service. The benediction, inserted in place of it, is taken from

---

tain other expressions taken from the Scottish Prayer-book of Laud.
* The result of the patch-work," says Bunsen. "Is (with a little grammatical inaccuracy) the following remarkable prayer." (Then follows the prayer as found in the Prayer-book of the Protestant Episcopal Church.) Vol. ii. p. 198.
† Eutaxia, p. 46. Preface to Lutheran Liturgy.

the Directory, and besides being in the very words of Scripture, has the advantage of rising into a solemn doxology of both minister and people at the close.

Sect. IX. *The Revised Baptismal Services.*

The Baptismal offices form a class of initiatory rites and services by means of which the children of the Church and converts from the world may be personally trained for the communion of the faithful. As here arranged, they contain the Directory inserted as literally as possible in place of the English Rubric, and will be found to be substantially in agreement with primitive and Presbyterian usage.

The *Order of Baptism of Infants* is simply our Baptismal Directory interwoven with appropriate forms or examples of each part of the service, originally derived in part from the ancient office, and in part from the formulary of Bucer and Melancthon, and afterwards subjected at first to the Calvinistic revision of 1552, and finally to the Presbyterian revision of 1661. The effect of these emendations has been, 1. The abolition of the office of Sponsors or Pro-parents, except in the anomalous cases mentioned in the last rubric; 2. The careful removal of expressions declaring the absolute and invariable regeneration of children in baptism; 3. The exclusion of chrism, the sign of the cross, and other superstitious ceremonies practised in the mediæval ritual. The Presbyterian revisers were willing that the use of the sign of the cross should be left free to the choice of the parents; but the phrase in our Directory, "without adding any other ceremony," seems to allow no such option. The alterations and amendments express the sense of our standards in their own language or in that of their framers, as far as can be, and the whole office, whether used as a model or as a fixed form, is suited to redeem this Sacrament from the practical neglect into which it has fallen, both as to its doctrine and the mode of administration.*

---

* For the sources of this form, see the Westminster and American Directory and Confession of Faith, the Presbyterian Exceptions and Rejoinder. Baxter's Reformed Liturgy the Proposed Alterations of

THE REVISED BAPTISMAL SERVICES. 129

The *Catechism*, defined "an instruction to be learned by baptized children and others before they come to the Communion," belongs to a class of strictly Protestant formularies which sprang up in great numbers at the Reformation, and were designed to ensure the early indoctrination of the rising generation. They proceed upon the principle of the catechetical schools in the primitive Church, and the Sunday-schools in the modern Church, and are a private and laic mode of teaching, as distinguished from the more public and official preaching of the Word. The need of a Larger Catechism, to be added to that which Cranmer placed in the Prayer-book, and used for the instruction of persons of riper years, was very soon felt, and several manuals of the foreign Reformers came into use, among them the Larger and Shorter Catechisms of Calvin, which were ordered by statute to be taught in the University of Oxford as late as 1578.* The meagreness of the Prayer-book Catechism led the Presbyterians to propose a number of amendments, in which it is plain they had before their minds those Westminster models which form our only authorized expositions of Christian doctrine. And we have therefore complied with both authorities by inserting the Creed, the Decalogue, and the Lord's Prayer, as the instruction for very young children, and the Westminster Catechism as the explication of those formularies for the indoctrination of the more advanced catechumen. At the same time, however, we are free to admit that another and simpler and more personal form, somewhat on the model of that in the Prayer-book, with the emendations of the Presbyterian revisers, is a great desideratum; and nothing but an unwillingness to risk the introduction of a disturbing element has prevented the insertion of it in this edition.†

1668 and 1689, and the Presbyterian Liturgies of the Continent. Knox's Book of Common Order. Digest of Acts of the General Assembly.
  * Eutaxia, p. 196. Procter, p. 392.
  † After the Exceptions against the Catechism were presented, the argument was thus continued:
  Episcopalian Answer. "The Catechism is not intended as a whole

The Order of Admission to the Lord's Supper of Children Baptized and come to Years of Discretion, is the logical, and, in a normal state of the Church, would be the invariable sequel and complement of the Baptismal service and the Catechetical training. Such a form or rite was no doubt practised from the apostles' time, until at length it became magnified into the pseudo-sacrament called *Confirmation;* and even those Reformed Churches which have discarded the namé have still retained the thing in the shape of some usage, more or less ceremonial, by which baptized persons are publicly admitted to the Communion. The form here given is simply chap. ix. of the Directory, prefixed as a rubric to the English office, so amended by the Presbyterians as to preclude several grave errors. The principal points of difference are, 1. Candidates are not simply required to recite memoriter the Commandments, the Apostles' Creed, and the Lord's Prayer, but must "be free from scandal," and "be examined as to their knowledge and piety."* 2. The "officers of the church are the judges of their qualifications,"† and the act of their admission to the Communion is not restricted to

---

body of divinity, but as a comprehension of the articles of faith, and other doctrines most necessary to salvation; and being short, is fittest for children and common people, and, as it was thought, sufficient upon mature deliberation, and so is by us."

Presbyterian Rejoinder. "The Creed, Decalogue, and the Lord's Prayer, contain all that is absolutely necessary to salvation at least. If you intended no more, what need you make a Catechism? If you intend more, why have you no more? But except in the very words of the Creed, the essentials of Christianity are left out. If no explication is necessary, trouble them with no more than the text of the Creed, &c. If explication be necessary, let them have it; at least in a Larger Catechism fitter for the riper." Documents, p. 328.

* " We desire that the credible, approved profession of faith and repentance be made necessaries." Presbyterian Rejoinder.

† "There exists a difference between the traditionary views and practice of the Presbyterian and Congregational Churches with respect to the ability, the right, and the duty of church officers, of forming and affirming a positive official judgment upon the inward spiritual character of applicants for church privileges. The Congregationalists understand by 'credible profession,' the positive evidence of a religious experience which satisfies the official judges of the gracious state of the applicant. The Presbyterians understand by that phrase only an intelligent *profession* of true spiritual faith in Christ which is not contradicted by the life." Hodge's Outlines of Theology, p. 515.

any superior order of diocesan clergymen, but exercised as an ordinary ministerial function by the pastor in connection with the parochial presbytery or elders of the congregation.* 3. The ancient benedictory symbol of the imposition of hands upon the head of the candidate is neither enjoined nor forbidden, and if practised, would appear neither as an apostolic rite nor as a sacramental sign conveying special grace, but only as an ordinary pastoral blessing and token of religious consecration, that might accord with the spontaneous feeling of the parties at the moment. The office, thus amended, forms a natural link between the two sacraments of infant Baptism and adult Communion, and is fitted not only to exhibit the truth in contrast with the error of Confirmation as practised in the Roman and Anglican Churches, but also to magnify the Sacraments rather than to depreciate them, and to develope the organic life of the Church by its own normal increase.†

The *Order of Baptism for Adults and such as are out of the Visible Church*, is a comparatively modern office;

---

* Prelatical as distinguished from Presbyterial Confirmation, is not practised in the Greek Church or in the Lutheran Church, and as retained in the Anglican Church is most naturally regarded as a remnant of Romanism, and one of the fruitful sources of a false theory of the ministry and Sacraments which has pervaded both bodies." See Stanley's History of Eastern Church, p. 518.

† "This passage (Heb. vi. 2) abundantly testifies that this rite had its beginning from the apostles, which afterwards, however, was turned into superstition, as the world almost always degenerates into corruptions, even with regard to the best institutions. They have, indeed, contrived the fiction that it is a Sacrament by which the spirit of regeneration is conferred, a dogma by which they have mutilated baptism; for what was peculiar to it, they transferred to the imposition of hands! Let us then know that it was instituted by its first founders that it might be an appointed rite for prayer, as Augustine calls it. The profession of faith which youth made, after having passed the time of childhood, they indeed intended to confirm by this symbol, but they thought of nothing less than to destroy the efficacy of baptism. Wherefore the pure institution at this day ought to be retained, but the superstition removed. And this passage tends to confirm pedo-baptism; for why should the same doctrine be called as to some baptism. but as to others the imposition of hands, except that the latter, after having received baptism, were taught in the faith, so that nothing remained for them but the laying on of hands?" Calvin's Commentary on Hebrews, p. 134. See also Schaff's History of Apos. Church, p 584. Neander's Hist., vol. 1 p. 315.

although Adult, as well as Infant, Baptism doubtless prevailed in the Church of the apostles as it must still prevail in unevangelized communities. As here amended, it consists of rubrics taken from our standards, and illustrated by forms derived from the same sources which yielded the Order of Infant Baptism, with such additions and alterations as the difference between them requires.

SECT. X. *The Revised Occasional Services.*

Under the head of Occasional Services we may conveniently class such as do not enter statedly into the Public Services as congregational acts of worship, but grow out of the special *occasions* of Matrimony, Sickness, Death, and Burial, when the Church comes in contact with domestic and social life. They are in no sense Sacraments, though they proceed upon natural relations and instincts which are recognised in the Scriptures as of divine appointment, and which it is the mission of the Christian ministry to cherish, exalt, and sanctify. As here presented, they will be found to have been derived from the same liturgical sources, and through the same revisions, to which we owe the services already reviewed.

The *Form of Solemnization of Matrimony* is derived in part from the ancient office, and in part from the formularies of Melancthon, Bucer, and Lasco. The greater portion of it also appears in the Genevan liturgy of Knox and Whittingham. The introductory and concluding rubrics are taken from the Directory, and, together with the few emendations made in the text according to the Presbyterian Exceptions, serve to guard the rite on the one hand from the superstition which would exalt it into a church-sacrament, and on the other from the sensuality which would degrade it into a mere civil compact. Certain expressions also have been dropped, which, though scriptural and salutary, and deserving to be read and pondered, are in questionable taste as recited in a public service; while at the same time enough has been retained to inculcate the sacredness and purity of true marriage both upon Christians and upon unbelievers.

The *Order for the Visitation of the Sick* is almost entirely due to the ancient office, the Absolution being omitted as liable to be perverted to superstitious ends, and the rubrics so amended as to better accord with American customs. Whether used as a model upon which to construct sick-room devotions, or as a form in cases where any is desired or needed, its fitness as an office of consolation cannot be questioned.

The *Order for the Communion of the Sick*, which may properly be blended with or added to the preceding service, is simply the English form, prefaced with a rubric, which is in the words of an Act passed by the last General Assembly, and by which it will be sufficiently guarded from superstition and perversion.

The *Order for the Burial of the Dead* is also mainly derived from the ancient service, but has been freed from mediæval superstitions and unsafe expressions by the Protestant additions and Presbyterian emendations which it has received. The Words of Committal* are from Bucer, amended with phrases from the Advent Collect, and from Rev. xx. 13; and the Prayers after Burial were added at the Calvinistic revision in 1552, and in the unmutilated form, in which they are here retained, bear internal evidence of their origin.†

The Presbyterian Exceptions also have been carefully applied, and the whole office thus rendered "consistent with the largest rational charity" towards the dead, as well as with that "instruction and comfort of the living," for which it is universally acknowledged to be so beautifully fitted.

Sect. XI. *The Additional Services.*

Besides domestic occasions for the exercise of the pastoral or ministerial function, there will arise other, more public emergencies, when the Church comes in

---

* The use of these words, after some discussion, was decided to be allowable by the Westminster Assembly. See Lightfoot's Journal.
† Compare also with the "Forme and Maner of Buriall usit in the Kirk of Montrois." Published by Wodrow Society. Miscellany, vol. i.

contact with the State; and the forms suited to them must vary according to the social usages or civil laws which prevail in different countries. To this class belong the *Additional Services* in this edition, printed in different type, as a supplement to the ordinary Prayer-book, and designed to adapt it more completely to the political and religious peculiarities of American society. They are taken from a Manual lately prepared by the editor, and examined and recommended by a number of clergymen of national reputation in the different Christian denominations of the country, and are, as far as possible, a compilation from the Holy Scriptures, the ancient liturgies, and the modern formularies of the Reformed Churches; the few examples not afforded by such sources having been composed out of scriptural and liturgical expressions after the same models. Although free from sectarian peculiarities, and compiled before the idea of this Prayer-book was formed, their addition to it may give it greater fulness and fitness, if not for actual use, yet at least as a help toward something better.*

---

* "A Manual of Worship, suitable to be used in Legislative and other Public Bodies, in the Army and Navy, and in Military and Naval Academies, Asylums, Hospitals, &c. Compiled from the Forms and in accordance with the Common Usages of all Christian Denominations."

RECOMMENDATION.

"The undersigned cordially unite in recommending this MANUAL OF WORSHIP as suitable for discretionary use in National and State Legislatures, in the Army and Navy, and in Military and Naval Institutions, in cases where our own respective rules and customs of worship cannot be exclusively maintained."

REV. ALBERT BARNES, Pastor of the First Presbyterian Church, (N. S.,) Philadelphia.
REV. II. W. BELLOWS, D. D., Minister to the First Congregational Church, (Unitarian,) New York.
REV. H. A. BOARDMAN. D. D, Pastor of the Tenth Presbyterian Church, (O. S.,) Philadelphia.
REV. CHARLES D COOPER, D. D., Rector of St. Philip's Church, (Episcopal,) Philadelphia.
REV. J. B. DALES, D. D., Pastor of the First United Presbyterian Church, Philadelphia.
REV. THOMAS DE WITT, D. D., Pastor of Collegiate Reformed Dutch Church, New York.
REV. J. P. DURBIN, D. D., Methodist Episcopal Church, New York.

THE ADDITIONAL SERVICES. 135

The *Form of Visitation of Mourners* is a social service, neither public nor domestic, strictly speaking, though it corresponds somewhat to the *Visitation of the Sick.* Its chief warrant, however, is the existing usage of having an office of devotion at the house of the deceased person, before proceeding to the church or to the grave, or in cases where it is not convenient or desirable for all the company to attend either of those services. On such informal occasions, the practice of reading aptly chosen portions of Scripture, and accompanying them with a brief address, if need be, and suitable petitions, has been found more acceptable than set lessons and collects, or than the opposite extreme of desultory exhortation and prayer.

The *Forms of Public Humiliation* and *Public Thanksgiving,* like the English state-services, are modelled upon the Order of the Daily and Sunday Offices, and may be either blended with or added to corresponding portions of those offices, as circumstances will dictate. The examples given are mainly of early English origin, with such modern emendations and additions as our political system demands; and it is believed that they comprise all the ordinary public vicissitudes which will

---

Rev. H. B. Hackett, D. D., Prof. in Newton (Baptist) Theological Institution. Mass

Rev. H. Harbaugh, D. D., Pastor of St. John's Church, (German Reformed,) Lebanon. Pa.

Rev. Charles Hodge, D. D., Professor of Theology, Princeton, New Jersey.

Rev. C. P. Krauth, D. D., Evangelical Lutheran Church, Philadelphia.

Right Rev. C. P. McIlvaine, D. D., D. C. L., Protestant Episcopal Church, Diocese of Ohio.

Right Rev. Alonzo Potter, D. D., LL. D., Protestant Episcopal Church. Diocese of Pennsylvania.

Rev. Barnas Sears, D. D., President of Brown University, Providence, R. I.

Rev. Thomas H Stockton, D. D., Methodist Protestant Church.

Bev. Thatcher Thayer, D.D., Pastor of the Congregational Church, Newport, R. I.

Rev. Jos. P. Thompson, D. D., Pastor of the Tabernacle (Congregational) Church, New York.

Rev. William R. Williams, D. D., Pastor of the Baptist Church, Amity Street, New York.

Rev. Theodore D. Woolsey, D. D., LL.D., President of Yale College, New Haven, Conn.

be likely to become, by appointment of the civil authority, an occasion either of humiliation or of thanksgiving.

The *Forms of Daily Prayer to be used in Legislatures, in the Army and Navy, in Schools and Families*, and other like recurrent occasions, are examples of a class of devotions, incident to civil and social life, for which the Prayer-book does not make adequate provision, as is shown by the numerous manuals which are issued to meet the want. The peculiarity of those here given is, that they are derived from catholic sources, and framed upon scriptural and liturgical models.

The *Various Prayers* and *Various Thanksgivings*, to be used in connection with the immediately preceding forms, or in the Daily or Sunday Office, as the special occasion will require, correspond to the miscellany usually placed after the Litany, but differ from them in being more numerous and various, and therefore too unwieldy a collection to be inserted in the midst of the ordinary service. They also are mainly classic in their origin and style, and may serve either as samples or as set forms, by means of which public, social, or private worship may be varied and adapted to the different emergencies and vicissitudes of human life.

The date and authorship of these forms, as far as ascertainable, will appear in our *General Index to the Historical Sources of the Prayer-book*, to which we must also refer the reader for a variety of other minute information respecting its contents, which could not be included in our previous review without pedantic and wearisome citations at every step of our progress. The accuracy of the Index, in any particular case, can easily be tested by referring to the authorities already quoted.

APPENDIX I.

A CHRONOLOGICAL LIST OF THE PRINCIPAL HISTORICAL AND LITURGICAL DOCUMENTS CONNECTED WITH THE COMPILATION AND REVISION OF THE PRAYER-BOOK, AND USED IN THE PREPARATION OF THIS EDITION.

The following List may sufficiently exhibit, at one view, the literary history of the Prayer-book, but comprises only such writings as are most authoritative in deciding questions relating to it, without pretending to include the numerous collateral works in the shape of histories, expositions, editions, and versions to which it has given rise, and which by themselves form a bibliography too extensive to be brought within the limits of this treatise.

King Edward's First Prayer-book (1549.)

The Latin Breviary, Missal, and Ritual.
The English Litany of Henry the Eighth.
The German Reformation-book of Bucer and Melancthon, prepared for Hermann, Elector of Cologne.
The English "Order of Communion."

King Edward's Second Prayer-book (1552.)

Calvin's Letters to the Lord Protector, to King Edward the Sixth, and to Bucer, urging further Reformation.
Bucer's Censura of the Prayer-book.
The Calvinistic Liturgy of Pollanus.
The Calvinistic Liturgy of Lasco.
King Edward's Prymer, or Book of Private Prayer.
Original Works and Letters of the English Reformers, collected by the Parker Society.

The Frankfort Prayer-book (1553.)

Brief Discourse of the Troubles at Frankfort, by Knox and Whittingham.
Original Letters and Works of the English Exiles at Frankfort.
Knox's Book of Common Order for the English Church at Geneva.

Queen Elizabeth's Prayer-book (1558.)

The Litany used in the Queen's Chapel.
Original Works and Letters of Elizabethan Reformers
The Puritan Editions of the Prayer-book.

The Prayer-book of King James I. (1603.)

The Millenary Petition for Revision.
Alterations or Explanations made in 1604.

The Prayer-book of Charles I. (1639.)

Archbishop Laud's Prayer-book for Scotland.
The Parliamentary Committee's Considerations upon the Book of Common Prayer.
The Parliamentary Order for Revision of the Liturgy.
The Calvinistic and Knoxian Liturgies before the Parliamentary Assembly of Divines.
The Westminster Assembly's Directory for Public Worship.

The Prayer-book of Charles II. (1661.)

Declaration of King Charles II. from Breda.
Interview of the Presbyterian Ministers with King Charles II. at Breda.
Discourse of the Ministers with King Charles II. in London.
The First Address and Proposals of the Ministers.

LIST OF AUTHORITIES. 139

Archbishop Usher's Model of Church Government.

Requests verbally presented to King Charles II. in consequence of the Act for restoring the English Clergy.

The Bishops' Answer to the First Proposals of the London Ministers, who attempted the work of reconcilement.

A Defence of our Proposals to His Majesty for Agreement in Matters of Religion.

His Majesty's Declaration to all his loving subjects of his kingdom of England and dominion of Wales concerning Ecclesiastical affairs.

The Petition of the Ministers to the King upon the first draft of his Declaration.

Alterations in the Declaration proposed by the Ministers.

Humble and grateful acknowledgment of some Ministers of London for the Declaration.

A Proclamation prohibiting all unlawful and seditious meetings and conventicles under pretence of religious worship.

The King's Warrant for the Conference at the Savoy.

The Exceptions against the Book of Common Prayer.

The Answer of the Bishops to the Exceptions of the Ministers.

The Petition for peace and concord presented to the Bishops with the proposed Reformation of the Liturgy.

The Rejoinder of the Ministers to the Answer of the Bishops.

Paper offered by Bishop Cosins, and Answer thereto.

The Discussion on Kneeling at the Lord's Supper.

The Discussion on the Sinfulness of the Liturgy.

The Reply to the Bishops' Disputants which was not answered.

Petition to the King at the close of the Conference.

The Act of Uniformity, 14 Car. ii. cap. 4.

Efforts of Presbyterian Ministers to have the King's Declaration of October, 1660, enacted.

Extracts from Journals of Parliament relating to the passing of the Act of Uniformity.

The Six Hundred Alterations made in the Book of Common Prayer by Convocation, and adopted by Parliament.

The Publication of the Book of Common Prayer.

The King's Declaration of the 27th of December, 1662.

Proceedings in Parliament upon the King's Declaration of 26th December, 1662.

The Conventicle Act, 1664; 16 Car. ii. cap. 4.

The Five Mile Act, 17 Car. ii. cap. 2.

The Conventicle Act, 1670; 22 Car. ii. cap. 1.

The Test Act, 25 Car. ii. cap. 2.

The Prayer-book of King William III.

Proposals for the Comprehension of the Presbyterians, and Indulgence to the Independents, between Bishops Stillingfleet, and Tillotson, etc., and Drs. Bates, Manton, and Baxter.

Declaration of William, Prince of Orange, to endeavor a good agreement between the Church of England and Protestant Dissenters.

Alterations in the Book of Common Prayer prepared by the Royal Commissioners for the Revision of the Liturgy in 1689.

The Toleration Act, 1 Guil. et Mar.

APPENDIX II.

THE PRESBYTERIAN EXCEPTIONS AGAINST THE BOOK OF COMMON PRAYER,

PRESENTED AT THE SAVOY CONFERENCE, A. D. 1661.

From the preceding list of authorities we select, for the reasons given in chap. viii., the following document, and here present it, not only as the basis of this edition, but as a historical nucleus of all previous and subsequent editions and revisions, as will appear in the notes which we have collated from the different authorities dating before and after it. The references are to pages in this treatise, which, in connection with corresponding portions of the Prayer-book, will show the manner in which these Exceptions have been applied.

ACKNOWLEDGING with all humility and thankfulness, his majesty's most princely condescension and indulgence, to very many of his loyal subjects, as well in his majesty's most gracious Declaration, as particularly in this present commission, issued forth in pursuance thereof; we doubt not but the right reverend bishops, and all the rest of his majesty's commissioners intrusted in this work, will, in imitation of his majesty's most prudent and Christian moderation and clemency, judge it their duty (what we find to be the apostles' own practice) in a special manner to be tender of the churches' peace, to bear with the infirmities of the weak, and not to please themselves, nor to measure the consciences of other men by the light and latitude of their own, but seriously and readily to consider and advise of such expedients as may most conduce to the healing of our breaches, and uniting those that differ.

And albeit we have a high and honorable esteem of

those godly and learned bishops and others, who were the first compilers of the public liturgy, and do look upon it as an excellent and worthy work, for that time, when the Church of England made her first step out of such a mist of popish ignorance and superstition wherein it formerly was involved; yet, considering that all human works do gradually arrive at their maturity and perfection, and this in particular, being a work of that nature, hath already admitted several emendations since the first compiling thereof:—

It cannot be thought any disparagement or derogation either to the work itself, or to the compilers of it, or to those who have hitherto used it, if after more than a hundred years, since its first composure, such further emendations be now made therein as may be judged necessary for satisfying the scruples of a multitude of sober persons, who cannot at all (or very hardly) comply with the use of it, as now it is, and may best suit with the present times after so long an enjoyment of the glorious light of the gospel, and so happy a reformation: especially considering that many godly and learned men have from the beginning all along earnestly desired the alteration of many things therein; and very many of his majesty's pious, peaceable, and loyal subjects, after so long a discontinuance of it, are more averse from it than heretofore; the satisfying of whom (as far as may be) will very much conduce to that peace and unity which is so much desired by all good men, and so much endeavored by his most excellent majesty.*

And therefore, in pursuance of this his majesty's most gracious commission, for the satisfaction of tender consciences, and the procuring of peace and unity amongst ourselves, we judge meet to propose,

I. First, that all the prayers and other materials of

---

* This Preface, in which a hundred years of grievance and protest find utterance, was warmly discussed, paragraph by paragraph, in the Episcopalian *Answer* and Presbyterian *Rejoinder;* and though its lofty conservatism and catholicity were disregarded by the English prelates in the day of their power, yet its spirit still lives in the liberal and spiritual portion of the Church of England, and cannot but increase in the corresponding class of American Episcopalians in proportion as the common enemy of ritualism shall force them into closer practical union with their hereditary Presbyterian allies.

the liturgy may consist of nothing *doubtful* or *questioned* amongst pious, learned, and orthodox persons, inasmuch as the professed end of composing them is for the declaring of the unity and consent of all who join in the public worship; it being too evident that the limiting of church-communion to things of *doubtful disputation*, hath been in all ages the ground of schism and separation, according to the saying of a learned person.*

"To load our public forms with the private fancies upon which we differ, is the most sovereign way to perpetuate schism to the world's end. Prayer, confession, thanksgiving, reading of the Scriptures, and administration of the sacraments in the plainest and simplest manner, were matter enough to furnish out a sufficient liturgy, though nothing either of private opinion, or of church-pomp, of garments, or prescribed gestures, of imagery, of music, of matter concerning the dead, of many superfluities which creep into the Church under the name of *order* and *decency*, did interpose itself. To charge churches and liturgies with things unnecessary, was the first beginning of all superstition, and when scruple of conscience began to be made or pretended, then schism began to break in. If the special guides and fathers of the Church would be a little sparing of incumbering churches with superfluities, or not over-rigid, either in reviving obsolete customs, or imposing new, there would be far less cause of schism or superstition; and all the inconvenience were likely to ensue would be but this, they should in so doing yield a little to the imbecility of their inferiors; a thing which St. Paul would never have refused to do. Meanwhile, wheresoever false or suspected opinions are made a piece of church-liturgy, he that separates is not the schismatic; for it is alike unlawful to make profession of known or suspected falsehood, as to put in practice unlawful or suspected action."

---

* In this first exception is presented that ideal of orthodoxy blended with charity, authority with liberty, and unity with variety, which Presbyterian churches, not only in England, but in all countries, have steadfastly pursued, oftentimes, as in this instance, at the expense of their worldly interests.

II. Further, we humbly desire that it may be seriously considered, that as our first Reformers out of their great wisdom did at that time so compose the liturgy as to win upon the papists, and to draw them into their church-communion, by varying as little as they well could from the Romish forms before in use: so whether in the present constitution, and state of things amongst us, we should not, according to the same rule of prudence and charity, have our liturgy so composed as to gain upon the judgments and affection of all those who, in the substantials of the Protestant religion, are of the same persuasions with ourselves: inasmuch as a more firm union and consent of all such, as well in worship as in doctrine, would greatly strengthen the Protestant interest against all those dangers and temptations which our intestine divisions and animosities do expose us unto from the common adversary.*

III. That the repetitions, and responsals of the clerk and people, and the alternate reading of the psalms and hymns, which cause a confused murmur in the congregation, whereby what is read is less intelligible, and therefore unedifying, may be omitted: the minister being appointed for the people in all public services appertaining unto God, and the Holy Scriptures, both of the Old and New Testament, intimating the people's part in public prayer to be only with silence and reverence to attend thereunto, and to declare their consent in the close by saying *Amen.*†

IV. That in regard the litany (though otherwise containing in it many holy petitions) is so framed that the petitions for a great part are uttered only by the people.

---

* An exception first raised at Frankfort in 1555, renewed at Hampton Court in 1603, adopted in the Westminster Assembly in 1645, disputed in the Episcopalian Answer, re-affirmed in the Presbyterian Rejoinder, partially conceded in 1668 by the Episcopalian Proposals for the Comprehension of the Presbyterians, and practically guaranteed in 1689 by the Act of Toleration.

† First broached at Frankfort. Practised for a century afterwards by the English Puritans. Authorized by the Parliamentary Assembly. Negatived in the Answer. Re-affirmed in the Rejoinder. Made illegal by the Act of Uniformity, and finally allowed by the Act of Toleration. Partially adopted by the American Episcopalians Applied, pp. 58, 84.

which we think not to be so consonant to Scripture, which makes the minister the mouth of the people to God in prayer, the particulars thereof may be composed into one solemn prayer to be offered by the minister unto God for the people.*

V. That there be nothing in the liturgy which may seem to countenance the observation of Lent as a religious fast; the example of Christ fasting forty days and nights being no more imitable, nor intended for the imitation of a Christian, than any other of his miraculous works were, or than Moses his forty days' fast was for the Jews; and the act of Parliament, 5 Eliz., forbidding abstinence from flesh to be observed upon any other than a politic consideration, and punishing all those who, by preaching, teaching, writing, or open speeches, shall notify that the forbearing of flesh is of any necessity for the saving of the soul, or that it is the service of God, otherwise than as other politic laws are.†

VI. That the religious observation of saints' days, appointed to be kept as holy-days, and the vigils thereof, without any foundation (as we conceive) in Scripture, may be omitted. That if any be retained, they may be called festivals, and not holy-days, nor made equal with the Lord's day, nor have any peculiar service appointed for them, nor the people be upon such days forced wholly to abstain from work, and that the names of all others now inserted in the Calendar, which are not in the first and second books of Edward the Sixth, may be left out.‡

VII. That the gift of prayer, being one special qualification for the work of the ministry bestowed by Christ

---

* First questioned at Frankfort Disputed in the Answer. Defended in the Rejoinder. Left indifferent in this edition.
† Proposed in the Westminster Assembly. Denied in the Answer. Defended in the Rejoinder. Conceded by the English Episcopalians in the Commission of 1689. Adopted by the American Episcopalians in the Convention of 1786. Applied. P. 116.
‡ Partially conceded by the Episcopalians in 1641. Made an appendix to the Westminster Directory in 1646. Refused in the Answer. Left indifferent in the Rejoinder. Dropped from the American Directory. Partially adopted in the American Episcopalian Prayer book. Applied. P. 116.

in order to the edification of his Church, and to be exercised for the profit and benefit thereof, according to its various and emergent necessity; it is desired that there may be no such imposition of the liturgy, as that the exercise of that gift be thereby totally excluded in any part of public worship. And further, considering the great age of some ministers and infirmities of others, and the variety of several services oft-times concurring upon the same day, whereby it may be inexpedient to require every minister at all times to read the whole, it may be left to the discretion of the minister to omit part of it, as occasion shall require; which liberty we find to be allowed even in the First Common Prayer-book of Edward VI.*

VIII. That in regard of the many defects which have been observed in that version of the Scriptures which is used throughout the liturgy (manifold instances whereof may be produced, as in the epistle for the first Sunday after Epiphany, taken out of Romans xii. 1, "Be ye changed in your shape;" and the epistle for the Sunday next before Easter, taken out of Philippians ii. 5, "Found in his apparel as a man;" as also the epistle for the fourth Sunday in Lent, taken out of the fourth of the Galatians, "Mount Sinai is Agar in Arabia, and bordereth upon the city which is now called Jerusalem;" the epistle for St. Matthew's day, taken out of the second epistle of Corinth, and the iv*th*, "We go not out of kind;" the gospel for the second Sunday after Epiphany, taken out of the second of John, "When men be drunk;" the gospel for the third Sunday in Lent, taken out of the xi*th* of Luke, "One house doth fall upon another;" the gospel for the Annunciation, taken out of the first of Luke, "This is the sixth month which was called barren:" and many other places,) we therefore desire, instead thereof, the new translation allowed by authority may alone be used †

---

* Practised for a century before by the Puritans. Authorized by the Parliamentary Assembly of Divines. Refused in the Answer. Defended in the Rejoinder. Forbidden by the Act of Uniformity. Allowed by the Act of Toleration. Practised, to some extent, by "Evangelical" Episcopalians. Guaranteed by the Directory.

† Conceded by the Episcopalians. Adopted in all subsequent Prayer-books throughout, except in the Commandments and the Psalter. Applied in the Commandments.

IX. That inasmuch as the holy Scriptures are able to make us wise unto salvation, to furnish us throughly unto all good works, and contain in them all things necessary, either in doctrine to be believed, or in duty to be practised; whereas divers chapters of the apocryphal books appointed to be read, are charged to be in both respects of dubious and uncertain credit: it is therefore desired, that nothing be read in the church for lessons, but the holy Scriptures of the Old and New Testament.*

X. That the minister be not required to rehearse any part of the liturgy at the communion-table, save only those parts which properly belong to the Lord's Supper; and that at such times only when the said holy Supper is administered.†

XI. That as the word "minister," and not priest or curate, is used in the Absolution, and in divers other places; it may throughout the whole book be so used instead of those two words; and that instead of the word "Sunday," the word "Lord's day" may be everywhere used.‡

XII. Because singing of psalms is a considerable part of public worship, we desire that the version set forth and allowed to be sung in churches may be amended; or that we may have leave to make use of a purer version.§

XIII. That all obsolete words in the Common Prayer, and such whose use is changed from their first significancy, as "aread" used in the gospel for the Monday and Wednesday before Easter; "Then opened he their

---

* First proposed at Hampton Court. Queried by the Episcopalians in 1641. Adopted by the Westminster Presbyterians. Discussed in the Answer and Rejoinder. Conceded by the Episcopalian Commissioners of 1668 and 1689. Retained in the American Confession of Faith. Applied. P. 94.

† First proposed by Bucer in 1549. Advocated by the Elizabethan Puritans. Maintained by the Episcopalians in 1641. Denied in the Answer. Defended in the Rejoinder. Applied. P. 107.

‡ Conceded by the Episcopalian Commissioners in 1689. Applied as far as now practicable. P. 107.

§ This Exception does not refer to the prose Psalter, but to Psalms in metre. See Answer and Rejoinder, and p. 92.

wits," used in the gospel for Easter Tuesday, &c ; may be altered unto other words generally received and better understood.*

XIV. That no portions of the Old Testament, or of the Acts of the Apostles, be called "epistles," and read as such.†

XV. That whereas throughout the several offices, the phrase is such as presumes all persons (within the communion of the church) to be regenerated, converted, and in an actual state of grace, (which, had ecclesiastical discipline been truly and vigorously executed, in the exclusion of scandalous and obstinate sinners, might be better supposed; but there having been, and still being a confessed want of that, (as in the liturgy is acknowledged,) it cannot be rationally admitted in the utmost latitude of charity :) we desire that this may be reformed.‡

XVI. That whereas orderly connection of prayers, and of particular petitions and expressions, together with a competent length of the forms used, are tending much to edification, and to gain the reverence of people to them; there appears to us too great a neglect of both, of this order, and of other just laws, of method.

PARTICULARLY.

1. The collects are generally short, many of them consisting but of one, or at most two sentences of petition; and these generally ushered in with a repeated mention of the name and attributes of God ; and presently concluding with the name and merits of Christ ; whence are caused many unnecessary intercisions and abruptions which, when many petitions are to be offered at the same time, are neither agreeable to scriptural examples, nor suited to the gravity and seriousness of that holy duty.§

---

* Conceded and generally adopted in the Prayer-book.
† Partially conceded and adopted.
‡ Urged by Bucer in 1549, and by th Puritans from the beginning. Enjoined by the Westminster formularies. Discussed in the Answer and Rejoinder without result. Conceded and proposed in 1668, and 1698. Carefully applied throughout this edition.
§ Denied in the Answer, but partially conceded and adopted in the Proposed Collects of 1698.

2. The prefaces of many collects have not any clear and special respect to the following petitions; and particular petitions are put together, which have not any due order, nor evident connection one with another, nor suitableness with the occasions upon which they are used, but seem to have fallen in rather casually, than from an orderly contrivance.

It is desired, that instead of those various collects, there may be one methodical and entire form of prayer composed out of many of them.*

XVII. That whereas the public liturgy of a church should in reason comprehend the sum of all such sins as are ordinarily to be confessed in prayer by the church, and of such petitions and thanksgivings as are ordinarily by the church to be put up to God, and the public catechisms or systems of doctrine, should summarily comprehend all such doctrines as are necessary to be believed, and these explicitly set down; the present liturgy as to all these seems very defective.

PARTICULARLY.

1. There is no preparatory prayer in our address to God for assistance or acceptance; yet many collects in the midst of the worship have little or nothing else.†

2. The Confession is very defective, not clearly expressing original sin, nor sufficiently enumerating actual sins, with their aggravations, but consisting only of generals; whereas confession being the exercise of repentance, ought to be more particular.‡

3. There is also a great defect as to such forms of public praise and thanksgiving as are suitable to gospel-worship.§

4. The whole body of the Common-prayer also consisteth very much of mere generals: as, "to have our prayers heard—to be kept from all evil, and from all

---

* Denied, but afterwards adopted, in several examples, in both English and American Prayer-books. Pp. 99, 98.

† Disproved in the Answer. Not applied. P. 91.

‡ Discussed in the Answer and Rejoinder, but neither before nor afterwards. Not applied. P. 90.

§ Queried in the Answer, but finally admitted and remedied in all subsequent editions. Applied. P. 99.

enemies, and all adversity, that we might do God's will;" without any mention of the particulars in which these generals exist.

5. The Catechism is defective as to many necessary doctrines of our religion; some even of the essentials of Christianity not mentioned except in the Creed, and there not so explicit as ought to be in a catechism,*

XVIII. Because this liturgy containeth the imposition of divers ceremonies which from the first reformation have by sundry learned and pious men been judged unwarrantable, as,

1. That public worship may not be celebrated by any minister that dare not wear a surplice.

2. That none may baptize, nor be baptized, without the transient image of the cross, which hath at least the semblance of a sacrament of human institution, being used as an engaging sign in our first and solemn covenanting with Christ; and the duties whereunto we are really obliged by baptism being more expressly fixed to that airy sign than to this holy sacrament.

3. That none may receive the Lord's Supper that dare not kneel in the act of receiving; but the minister must exclude all such from the communion: although such kneeling not only differs from the practice of Christ and of his apostles, but (at least on the Lord's day) is contrary to the practice of the catholic church for many hundred years after, and forbidden by the most venerable councils that ever were in the Christian world. All which impositions are made yet more grievous by that subscription to their lawfulness which the canon exacts, and by the heavy punishment upon the non-observance of them which the act of uniformity inflicts.

And it being doubtful whether God hath given power unto men, to institute in his worship such mystical teaching signs, which not being necessary *in genere*, fall not under the rule of "doing all things decently, orderly, and to edification," and which once granted, will, upon the same reason, open a door to the arbitrary imposition of numerous ceremonies of which St. Augustine complained in his days; and the things in contro-

---

* See below. Exceptions against the Catechism

versy being in the judgment of the imposers confessedly indifferent, who do not so much as pretend any real goodness in them of themselves, otherwise than what is derived from their being imposed, and consequently the imposition ceasing, that will cease also, and the worship of God not become indecent without them:

Whereas, on the other hand, in the judgment of the opposers, they are by some held sinful, and unlawful in themselves: by others very inconvenient and unsuitable to the simplicity of gospel worship, and by all of them very grievous and burthensome, and therefore not at all fit to be put in balance with the peace of the church, which is more likely to be promoted by their removal than continuance: considering also how tender our Lord and Saviour himself is of weak brethren, declaring it much better for a man to have a "millstone hanged about his neck, and be cast into the depth of the sea, than to offend one of his little ones:" and how the apostle Paul (who had as great legislative power in the church as any under Christ) held himself obliged by that common rule of charity, "not to lay a stumbling block, or an occasion of offence before a weak brother, choosing rather not to eat flesh whilst the world stands" (though in itself a thing lawful) "than offend his brother for whom Christ died:" we cannot but desire that these ceremonies may not be imposed on them who judge such impositions a violation of the royalty of Christ, and an impeachment of his laws as insufficient, and are under the holy awe of that which is written, Deut. xii. 32; "What thing soever I command you, observe to do it; thou shalt not add thereto, nor diminish from it;" but that there may be either a total abolition of them, or at least such a liberty, that those who are unsatisfied concerning their lawfulness or expediency, may not be compelled to the practice of them, or subscription to them; but may be permitted to enjoy their ministerial function, and communion with the church, without them.

The rather because these ceremonies have for above an hundred years been the fountain of manifold evils in this church and nation, occasioning sad divisions between ministers and ministers, as also between ministers and people; exposing many orthodox, pious, and peaceable ministers to the displeasure of their rulers, casting them on the edge of the penal statutes, to the loss not only of their living and liberties, but also of their opportunities for the service of Christ and his church; and forcing people either to worship God in such a manner as their own consciences condemn, or doubt of, or else to forsake our assemblies, as thousands have done. And no better fruits than these can be looked for from the retaining and imposing of these ceremonies, unless we could presume that all his majesty's subjects should have the same subtilty of judgment to discern even to a ceremony how far the power of man extends in the things of God, which is not to be expected; or should yield obedience to all the impositions of men concerning them, without inquiring into the will of God, which is not to be desired.

We do therefore most earnestly entreat the right reverend fathers and brethren, to whom these papers are delivered, as they tender the glory of God, the honor of religion, the peace of the Church, the service of his majesty in the accomplishment of that happy union, which his majesty hath so abundantly testified his desires of, to join with us in importuning his most excellent majesty, that his most gracious indulgence, as to these ceremonies, granted in his royal Declaration, may be confirmed and continued to us and our posterities, and extended to such as do not yet enjoy the benefit thereof.*

XIX. As to that passage in his majesty's Commission, where we are authorized and required to compare the present liturgy with the most ancient liturgies which have been used in the Church in the purest and most primitive times; we have in obedience to his majesty's Commission, made inquiry, but cannot find any records

---

* These ceremonies were abandoned by the English Episcopalians at Frankfort; opposed by the Puritans at Hampton Court: minutely enjoined in the Scottish Prayer-book; abolished by the Parliamentary Assembly; defended in the Answer; deplored in the Rejoinder; left indifferent in the Proposed Prayer-book of 1668, and also to some extent in the Protestant Episcopal Prayer-book, and in this edition. Pp. 83, 84.

of known credit, concerning any entire forms of liturgy, within the first three hundred years, which are confessed to be as the most primitive, so the purest ages of the Church; nor any impositions of liturgies upon any national Church for some hundreds of years after. We find indeed some liturgical forms fathered upon St. Basil, St. Chrysostom, and St. Ambrose, but we have not seen any copies of them, but such as give us sufficient evidence to conclude them either wholly spurious, or so interpolated, that we cannot make a judgment which in them hath any primitive authority.*

Having thus in general expressed our desires, we come now to particulars, which we find numerous and of a various nature; some, we grant, are of inferior consideration, verbal rather than material, (which, were they not in the public liturgy of so famous a Church, we should not have mentioned,) others dubious and disputable, as not having a clear foundation in Scripture for their warrant: but some there be that seem to be corrupt, and to carry in them a repugnancy to the rule of the gospel; and therefore have administered just matter of exception and offence to many, truly religious and peaceable,—not of a private station only, but learned and judicious divines, as well of other reformed Churches as of the Church of England,—ever since the Reformation.

We know much hath been spoken and written by way of apology in answer to many things that have been objected; but yet the doubts and scruples of tender consciences still continue, or rather are increased. We do humbly conceive it therefore a work worthy of those wonders of salvation, which God hath wrought for his majesty now on the throne, and for the whole kingdom, and exceedingly becoming the ministers of the gospel of peace, with all holy moderation and tenderness to endeavor the removal of everything out of the worship of God which may justly offend or grieve the spirits of sober and godly people. The things themselves that

---

* Disputed in the Answer. Defended with a learned argument in the Rejoinder.

are desired to be removed, not being of the foundation of religion, nor the essentials of public worship, nor the removal of them any way tending to the prejudice of the Church or State; therefore their continuance and rigorous imposition can no ways be able to countervail the laying aside of so many pious and able ministers, and the unconceivable grief that will arise to multitudes of his majesty's most loyal and peaceable subjects, who upon all occasions are ready to serve him with their prayers, estates, and lives. For the preventing of which evils we humbly desire that these particulars following may be taken into serious and tender consideration.

CONCERNING MORNING AND EVENING PRAYER.

Rubric.	*Exception.*
That morning and evening prayer shall be used in the accustomed place of the church, chancel, or chapel, except it be otherwise determined by the ordinary of the place; and the chancel shall remain as in times past.	We desire that the words of the first rubric may be expressed as in the book established by authority of parliament 5 and 6 Edw. VI. thus: "The morning and evening prayer shall be used in such place of of the church, chapel, or chancel, and the minister

shall so turn him, as the people may best hear, and if there be any controversy therein, the matter shall be referred to the ordinary."*

Rubric.	*Exception.*
And here is to be noted, that the minister, at the time of the communion, and at other times, in his ministration shall use such ornaments in the church,	Forasmuch as this rubric seemeth to bring back the cope, albe, &c., and other vestments forbidden by the Common Prayer-book 5 and 6 Edw. VI. and so our rea-

---

* Substantially conceded by the Episcopalians in 1641. Refused in the Answer. Formally proposed by the Episcopalian Commissioners of 1698. The rubric is omitted in the Prot. Epis. Prayer-book, and in this edition.

THE PRESBYTERIAN EXCEPTIONS. 155

as were in use by authority of parliament, in the second year of the reign of Edward the Sixth, according to the act of parliament.

sons alleged against ceremonies under our eighteenth general exception, we desire it may be wholly left out.*

Rubric.

The Lord's Prayer after the absolution ends thus, "Deliver us from evil."

Exception.

We desire that these words,† "For thine is the kingdom, the power and the glory, for ever and ever. Amen," may be always added unto the Lord's prayer; and that this prayer may not be enjoined to be so often used in morning and evening service.

Rubric.

And at the end of every psalm throughout the year, and likewise in the end of *Benedictus, Benedicite, Magnificat,* and *Nunc Dimittis,* shall be repeated, "Glory be to the Father," &c.

Exception.

By this rubric, and other places in the Common Prayer-books, the *Gloria Patri* is appointed to be said six times ordinarily in every morning and evening service, frequently eight times in a morning, sometimes ten; which we think carries with it at least an appearance of that vain repetition which Christ forbids: for the avoiding of which appearance of evil, we desire it may be used but once in the morning, and once in the evening.‡

Rubric.

In such places where they do sing, there shall the Lessons be sung, in a

Exception.

The Lessons, and the Epistles, and Gospels, being for the most part nei-

---

* The history is the same as that of the preceding Exception.
† Conceded by the Episcopalians in 1641. Disputed in the Answer, but adopted in all subsequent Prayer-books, in most instances.
‡ Conceded by the Episcopalians in 1641. Refused in the Answer. Proposed by the Episcopalians in 1698. Applied. P. 92.

plain tune, and likewise the Epistle and Gospel. ther psalms nor hymns, we know no warrant why they should be sung in any place, and conceive that the distinct reading of them with an audible voice tends more to the edification of the church.*

Rubric.

Or this canticle, *Benedicite omnia opera.*

Exception.

We desire that some psalm or scripture hymn may be appointed instead of that apocryphal.†

IN THE LITANY.

Rubric.

From all fornication, and all other deadly sin.

Exception.

In regard that the wages of sin is death; we desire that this clause may be thus altered; "From fornication, and all other heinous, or grievous sins."‡

Rubric.

From battle, and murder, and sudden death.

Exception.

Because this expression of "sudden death" hath been so often excepted against, we desire, if it be thought fit, it may be thus read: "From battle and murder, and from dying suddenly, and unprepared."§

Rubric.

That it may please thee, to preserve all that travel by land or by water, all

Exception.

We desire the term "all" may be advised upon, as seeming liable to just ex-

---

* Proposed by the Episcopalians in 1641. Disputed in the Answer. Adopted in all subsequent Prayer books.

† Conceded by the Episcopalians in 1641. Refused in the Answer. Applied. P. 93.

‡ Conceded by the Episcopalians in 1641. Refused in the Answer. Defended in the Rejoinder.

§ First broached at Frankfort. Renewed at Hampton Court. Denied in the Answer. Conceded and proposed in 1608. Not Applied. P. 104.

women laboring with child, all sick persons, and young children, and to show thy pity upon all prisoners and captives.

ceptions; and that it may be considered, whether it may not better be put indefinitely, "those that travel," &c., rather than universally.*

THE COLLECT ON CHRISTMAS DAY.

Rubric.

Almighty God, which hast given us thy only begotten Son, to take our nature upon him, and this day to be born of a pure virgin, &c.

Exception.

We desire that in both collects the word "this day" may be left out, it being according to vulgar acceptation a contradiction.†

Rubric.

Then shall follow the collect of the Nativity, which shall be said continually unto new-years-day.

THE COLLECT FOR WHITSUNDAY.

Rubric.

God, which upon this day, &c.

Rubric.

The same collect to be read on Monday and Tuesday in Whitsun-week.

Rubric.

The two collects for St. John's day, and Innocent's, the collects for the first day in Lent, for the fourth

Exception.

We desire that these collects may be further considered and abated, as having in them divers

---

* Denied in the Answer. Defended in the Rejoinder.
† Conceded and substantially adopted in all subsequent Prayer books.

Sunday after Easter, for Trinity Sunday, for the sixth and twelfth Sunday after Trinity, for St. Luke's day, and Michaelmas day.*

things that we judge fit to be altered.

THE ORDER FOR THE ADMINISTRATION OF THE LORD'S SUPPER.

Rubric.

So many as intend to be partakers of the holy communion shall signify their names to the curate over night, or else in the morning before the beginning of morning prayer, or immediately after.

Exception.

The time here assigned for notice to be given to the minister is not sufficient.†

Rubric.

And if any of these be a notorious evil liver, the curate, having knowledge thereof, shall call him and advertise him in any wise not to presume to the Lord's table.

Exception.

We desire the ministers' power both to admit and keep from the Lord's table, may be according to his majesty's Declaration, 25th Oct., 1660, in these words: "The minister shall admit none to the Lord's supper till they have made a credible profession of their faith, and promised obedience to the will of God, according as is expressed in the considerations of the rubric before the catechism; and that all possible diligence be used for the instruction and reformation of scandalous offenders, whom the minister shall not suffer to partake of the Lord's table until they have openly declared themselves to have truly repented and amended their former

---

* Evaded in the Answer, but adopted in the Prayer-book.
† Queried by the Episcopalians in 1641. Conceded in the Answer and adopted.

naughty lives, as is partly expressed in the rubric, and more fully in the canons."*

Rubric.	Exception.
Then shall the priest rehearse distinctly all the ten commandments, and the people kneeling, shall after every commandment, ask God's mercy for transgressing the same.	We desire, 1. That the preface prefixed by God himself to the ten commandments may be restored.† 2. That the fourth commandment may be read as in Exod. xx., Deut. v., "He

blessed the Sabbath-day."‡

3. That neither minister nor people may be enjoined to kneel more at the reading of this than of other parts of Scriptures, the rather because many ignorant persons are thereby induced to use the ten commandments as a prayer.§

4. That, instead of those short prayers of the people intermixed with the several commandments, the minister, after the reading of all, may conclude with a suitable prayer.‖

Rubric.	Exception.
After the Creed, if there be no sermon, shall follow one of the homilies already set forth, or hereafter to be set forth by common authority.	We desire that the preaching of the word may be strictly enjoined, and not left so indifferent, at the administration of the sacraments; as also that ministers may not be bound to those things which are as yet but future and not in being.¶

---

* Conceded by the Episcopalians in 1641. Conceded in the Answer, and substantially adopted.
† Conceded, but not adopted.
‡ Ibid.
§ Refused in the Answer, but conceded and proposed in 1668. Left indifferent in this edition. P. 110
‖ See last note.
¶ Urged by the Puritans for a century. Denied in the Answer. Defended in the Rejoinder. Applied. P. 113.

After such sermon, homily, or exhortation, the curate shall declare, &c., and earnestly exhort them to remember the poor, say one or more of these sentences following.

Then shall the churchwardens, or some other by them appointed, gather the devotion of the people.

Two of the sentences here cited are apocryphal, and four of them more proper to draw out the people's bounty to their ministers, than their charity to the poor.*

Collection for the poor may be better made at or a little before the departing of the communicants.†

Exhortation.

We be come together at this time to feed at the Lord's supper, unto the which in God's behalf I bid you all that be here present, and beseech you, for the Lord Jesus Christ's sake, that ye will not refuse to come, &c.

If it be intended that these exhortations should be read at the communion, they seem to us to be unseasonable.‡

The way and means thereto is first to examine your lives and conversation; and if ye shall perceive your offences to be such as be not only against God, but also against your neighbors, then ye shall reconcile yourselves unto them, and be ready to make restitution and satisfaction.

And because it is requisite that no man should come to the holy communion but with a full trust in God's mercy and with a quiet conscience.

We fear this may discourage many from coming to the sacrament, who lie under a doubting and troubled conscience.§

---

* Refused in the Answer, but conceded partially in 1698. Applied. P. 121.

† Queried by the Episcopalians in 1641. Left indifferent in this edition.

‡ Disputed, but partially conceded and adopted.

§ Disputed in the Answer. Defended in the Rejoinder. Partially conceded in 1659. Applied. P. 121.

THE PRESBYTERIAN EXCEPTIONS. 161

[*Rubr.*] *Before the Confession.*

Then shall this general confession be made in the name of all those that are minded to receive the holy communion either by one of them, or else by one of the ministers, or by the priest himself.

We desire it may be made by the minister only.*

[*Rubr.*] *Before the Confession.*

Then shall the priest or the bishop (being present) stand up, and turning himself to the people, say thus.

Exception.

The minister turning himself to the people is most convenient throughout the whole ministration.†

[*Proper*] *Preface on Christmas day, and seven days after.*

Because thou didst give Jesus Christ, thine only Son, to be born as this day for us, &c.

First, we cannot peremptorily fix the nativity of our Saviour to this or that day particularly.‡ Secondly, it seems incongruous to affirm the birth of Christ and the descending of the Holy Ghost to be on this day for seven or eight days together.§

[*Proper Preface*] *Upon Whitsunday, and six days after.*

According to whose most true promise, the Holy Ghost came down this day from heaven.

Prayer before that which is at the consecration.

Grant us that our sinful

We desire that, whereas

---

* Queried by the Episcopalians in 1641. Partially conceded and adopted. Applied.
† Queried by the Episcopalians in 1641. Refused in the Answer. Defended in the Rejoinder. Applied.
‡ Denied in the Answer. Proved in the rejoinder.
§ Not noticed in the Answer, but adopted in the Prayer-book.

L

bodies may be made clean by his body, and our souls washed through his most precious blood.

these words seem to give a greater efficacy to the blood than to the body of Christ, they may be altered thus, "That our sinful souls and bodies may be cleansed through his precious body and blood."*

Prayer at the consecration.

Hear us, O merciful Father, &c., who in the same night that he was betrayed took bread, and when he had given thanks, he brake it, and gave to his disciples, saying, Take, eat, &c.

We conceive that the manner of the consecrating of the elements is not here explicit and distinct enough, and the minister's breaking of the bread is not so much as mentioned.†

Rubric.

Then shall the minister first receive the communion in both kinds, &c., and after deliver it to the people in their hands, kneeling; and when he delivereth the bread, he shall say, "The body of our Lord Jesus Christ, which was given for thee, preserve thy body and soul unto everlasting life, and take and eat this in remembrance," &c.

We desire, that at the distribution of the bread and wine to the communicants, we may use the words of our Saviour as near as may be, and that the minister be not required to deliver the bread and wine into every particular communicant's hand, and to repeat the words to each one in the singular number, but that it may suffice to speak them to divers jointly, according to our Saviour's example.‡

We also desire that the kneeling at the sacrament (it being not that gesture which the apostles used, though

---

* Disputed in the Answer. Defended in the Rejoinder. Conceded and proposed in 1668, and 1689. Applied. P. 123.
† Partially conceded. Fully applied. P. 124.
‡ Refused in the Answer. Defended in the Rejoinder. Applied. P. 125.

Christ was personally present amongst them, nor that which was used in the purest and primitive times of the church) may be left free, as it was 1 and 2 Edw. [VI,] "As touching kneeling, &c., they may be used or left as every man's devotion serveth, without blame."*

Rubric.	Exception.
And note that every parishioner shall communicate at the least three times in the year, of which Easter to be one, and shall also receive the sacraments and other rites, according to the order in this book appointed.	Forasmuch as every parishioner is not duly qualified for the Lord's supper, and those habitually prepared are not at all times actually disposed, but many may be hindered by the providence of God, and some by the distemper of their own spirits, we de-

sire this rubric may be either wholly omitted, or thus altered:—

"Every minister shall be bound to administer the sacrament of the Lord's supper at least thrice a year, provided there be a due number of communicants manifesting their desires to receive."†

And we desire that the following rubric in the Common Prayer-book, in 5 and 6 Edw. [VI,] established by law as much as any other part of the Common Prayer-book, may be restored for the vindicating of our church in the matter of kneeling at the sacrament (although the gesture be left indifferent:) "Although no order can be so perfectly devised but it may be of some, either for their ignorance and infirmity, or else of malice and obstinacy, misconstrued, depraved, and interpreted in a wrong part; and yet, because brotherly charity willeth that, so much as conveniently may be, offences should be taken away; therefore are we willing to do the same. Whereas it is ordained in the book of Common Prayer, in the administration of the Lord's supper,

---

* Maintained by Bucer in 1549. Partially conceded by the Episcopalians in 1641. Refused in the Answer. Defended in the Rejoinder. Conceded and proposed in 1668, and 1689.

† Conceded by the Episcopalians in 1641. Refused in the Answer. Conceded and proposed in 1689.

that the communicants kneeling should receive the holy communion, which thing being well meant for a signification of the humble and grateful acknowledging of the benefits of Christ given unto the worthy receivers, and to avoid the profanation and disorder which about the holy communion might else ensue, lest yet the same kneeling might be thought or taken otherwise, we do declare, that it is not meant thereby that any adoration is done, or ought to be done, either unto the sacramental bread or wine there bodily received, or unto any real and essential presence there being of Christ's natural flesh and blood: for as concerning the sacramental bread and wine, they remain still in their very natural substances, and therefore may not be adored; for that were idolatry to be abhorred of all faithful Christians: and as concerning the natural body and blood of our Saviour Christ, they are in heaven, and not here; for it is against the truth of Christ's natural body to be in more places than in one at one time."*

OF PUBLIC BAPTISM.

There being divers learned, pious, and peaceable ministers who not only judge it unlawful to baptize children whose parents both of them are atheists, infidels, heretics, or unbaptized, but also such whose parents are excommunicate persons, fornicators, or otherwise notorious and scandalous sinners; we desire they may not be enforced to baptize the children of such, until they have made due profession of their repentance.†

Before Baptism.

Rubric.	*Exception.*
Parents shall give notice over night, or in the morning.	We desire that more timely notice may be given.‡

---

* Procured by Knox. Approved by Bucer. Denied in the Answer, but partially adopted in the Prayer-book. Fully conceded, enlarged, and amended in 1689.

† Disputed in the Answer. Defended in the Rejoinder. Conceded and proposed in 1689. Applied.

‡ Denied in the Answer. Defended in the Rejoinder. Applied.

THE PRESBYTERIAN EXCEPTIONS. 165

Rubric.

And the godfathers, and the godmothers, and the people with the children, &c.

Exception.

Here is no mention of the parents, in whose right the child is baptized, and who are fittest both to dedicate it unto God, and to covenant for it: we do not know that any persons except the parents, or some others appointed by them, have any power to consent for the children, or to enter them into covenant. We desire it may be left free to parents, whether they will have sureties to undertake for their children in baptism or no.*

Rubric.

Ready at the font.

Exception.

We desire it may be so placed as all the congregation may best see and hear the whole administration.†

In the first Prayer.

By the baptism of thy well-beloved Son, &c., didst sanctify the flood Jordan, and all other waters. to the mystical washing away of sin, &c.

It being doubtful whether either the flood Jordan or any other waters were sanctified to a sacramental use, by Christ's being baptized, and not necessary to be asserted, we desire this may be otherwise expressed.‡

The Third Exhortation.

Do promise by you that be their sureties.

We know not by what right the sureties do promise and answer in the name of the infant: it seemeth to us also to countenance

---

* First proposed at Hampton Court. Refused in the Answer. Defended in the Rejoinder. Conceded and proposed in 1668 and 1689. Partially adopted in the American Episcopalian Prayer-book.
† First proposed by Bucer in 1549. Discussed. but left indifferent.
‡ Urged by Bucer in 1549. Conceded in 1641. Disputed in the Answer. Defended in the Rejoinder. Conceded and proposed in 1668 and 1689. Adopted in subsequent Prayer-books. Applied.

The Questions.
Dost thou forsake, &c.
Dost thou believe, &c.
Wilt thou be baptized, &c.

the Anabaptistical opinion of the necessity of an actual profession of faith and repentance in order to baptism. That such a profession may be required of parents in their own name, and now solemnly renewed when they present their children to baptism, we willingly grant: but the asking of one for another is a practice whose warrant we doubt of: and therefore we desire that the first two interrogatories may be put to the parents to be answered in their own names, and the last propounded to the parents or pro-parents thus, "Will you have this child baptized into this faith?"*

The second Prayer before Baptism.

May receive remission of [their] sins by spiritual regeneration.

This expression seeming inconvenient, we desire it may be changed into this; "May be regenerated and receive the remission of sins."†

In the Prayer after Baptism.

That it hath pleased thee to regenerate this infant by thy Holy Spirit.

We cannot in faith say, that every child that is baptized is "regenerated by God's Holy Spirit;" at least it is a disputable point, and therefore we desire it may be otherwise expressed.‡

---

* Suggested by Bucer in 1549. Urged at Hampton Court in 1603. Conceded and proposed in 1668 and 1689. Applied.
† Discussed in the Answer and Rejoinder. Conceded and proposed in 1668 and 1689. Applied.
‡ Disputed in the Answer. Defended in the Rejoinder. Conceded and proposed in 1668. Applied.

[*Rubric*] *after Baptism.*

Then shall the priest make a cross, &c.	Concerning the cross in baptism, we refer to our 18th general.*

OF PRIVATE BAPTISM.

We desire that baptism may not be administered in a private place at any time, unless by a lawful minister, and in the presence of a competent number: that where it is evident that any child hath been so baptized, no part of the administration may be reiterated in public, under any limitations: and therefore we see no need of any liturgy in that case.†

OF THE CATECHISM.‡

Catechism.	*Exception.*
1. *Quest.* What is your name, &c.	We desire these three first questions may be altered; considering that the far greater number of persons baptized within these twenty years last past, had no godfathers or godmothers at their baptism. The like to be done in the seventh question.
2. *Quest.* Who gave you that name?	
Ans. My godfathers and my godmothers in my baptism; wherein I was made a member of Christ, the child of God, and an inheritor of the kingdom of heaven.	
3. *Quest.* What did your godfathers and godmothers do for you in baptism?	We conceive it might be more safely expressed thus; " Wherein I was visibly admitted into the number of the members of Christ, the
[*Ans.* They did promise	

---

* Urged at Hampton Court in 1603. Queried by the Episcopalians in 1641. Refused in the Answer. Defended in the Rejoinder. Conceded and proposed in 1668 and 1689. Adopted in the American Prayer-books.

† Suggested by Bucer and at Hampton Court. Discussed in the Answer and Rejoinder. Conceded and proposed in 1668. Applied.

‡ The various changes proposed in the Catechism were discussed in the Answer and Rejoinder without result; and though virtually conceded and proposed in 1689, have never been adopted.

and vow three things in my name, &c.]

Of the Rehearsal of the Ten Commandments.
10. *Ans.* My duty towards God is to believe in him, &c.

children of God, and the heirs (rather than 'inheritors') of the kingdom of heaven."

We desire that the commandments be inserted according to the new translation of the Bible.

In this answer there seems to be particular respect to the several commandments of the first table, as in the following answer to those of the second. And therefore we desire it may be advised upon, whether 'to the last word of this answer may not be added, "particularly on the Lord's day," otherwise there being nothing in all this answer that refers to the fourth commandment.

14. *Quest.* How many sacraments hath Christ ordained, &c.?
Ans. Two only as generally necessary to salvation.

That these words may be omitted, and answer thus given; "Two only, baptism and the Lord's supper."

19. *Quest.* What is required of persons to be baptized?
Ans. Repentance, whereby they forsake sin; and faith, whereby they steadfastly believe the promises of God, &c.

20. *Quest.* Why then are infants baptized when by reason of their tender age they cannot perform them?
Ans. Yes: they do perform them by their sureties, who promise and vow them both in their names.

We desire that the entering infants into God's covenant may be more warily expressed, and that the words may not seem to found their baptism upon a really actual faith and repentance of their own; and we desire that a promise may not be taken for a performance of such faith and repentance: and especially, that it be not asserted that they perform these by the promise of their sureties, it being to the seed of believers that the covenant of God is made; and not (that we can find) to all that have such believing sureties, who are neither parents nor pro-parents of the child.

In the general we observe, that the doctrine of the sacraments which was added upon the conference at Hampton Court, is much more fully and particularly delivered than the other parts of the Catechism, in short answers fitted to the memories of children, and thereupon we offer it to be considered:—

First, Whether there should not be a more distinct and full explication of the Creed, the Commandments and the Lord's Prayer.

Secondly, Whether it were not convenient to add (what seems to be wanting) somewhat particularly concerning the nature of faith, of repentance, the two covenants, of justification, sanctification, adoption, and regeneration.

OF CONFIRMATION.

The last Rubric before the Catechism.

And that no man shall think that any detriment shall come to children by deferring of their confirmation, he shall know for truth, that it is certain by God's word that children, being baptized, have all things necessary for their salvation, and be undoubtedly saved.

Although we charitably suppose the meaning of these words was only to exclude the necessity of any other sacraments to baptized infants; yet these words are dangerous as to the misleading of the vulgar, and therefore we desire they may be expunged.*

Rubric after the Catechism.

So soon as the children can say in their mother-tongue the Articles of the Faith, the Lord's Prayer,

We conceive that it is not a sufficient qualification for confirmation, that children be able *memoriter*

---

* Conceded in 1641. Partially conceded in the Answer, but not adopted in the Prayer book. Defended in the Rejoinder. Adopted in the Protestant Episcopal Prayer-book.

and the Ten Commandments, and can answer such other questions of this short Catechism, &c., then shall they be brought to the bishop, &c., and the bishop shall confirm them.

to repeat the Articles of the Faith, commonly called the Apostles' Creed, the Lord's Prayer, and the Ten Commandments, and to answer to some questions of this short Catechism; for it is often found

that children are able to do all this at four or five years old. 2dly. It crosses what is said in the third reason of the first rubric before confirmation, concerning the usage of the church in times past, ordaining that confirmation should be ministered unto them that were of perfect age, that they being instructed in the Christian religion, should openly profess their own faith, and promise to be obedient to the will of God. And therefore, 3dly, we desire that none may be confirmed but according to his majesty's Declaration, viz., "That confirmation be rightly and solemnly performed by the information, and with the consent of the minister of the place."*

Rubric after the Catechism.

Then shall they be brought to the bishop by one that shall be his godfather or godmother.

This seems to bring in another sort of godfathers and godmothers, besides those made use of in baptism; and we see no need either of the one or the other.†

The Prayer before the Imposition of Hands.

Who hast vouchsafed to regenerate these thy servants by water and the Holy Ghost, and hast giv-

This supposeth that all the children who are brought to be confirmed have the Spirit of Christ,

---

* Urged by Bucer. Disputed in the Answer. Defended in the Rejoinder. Fully conceded and proposed in 1689. Applied.

† Discussed without result. Adopted in the Protestant Episcopal Prayer-book.

en unto them the forgiveness of all their sins.

and the forgiveness of all their sins; whereas a great number of children at that age, having committed many sins since their baptism, do show no evidence of serious repentance, or of any special saving grace; and therefore this confirmation (if administered to such) would be a perilous and gross abuse.*

Rubric before the Imposition of Hands.

Then the bishop shall lay his hand on every child severally.

This seems to put a higher value upon confirmation than upon baptism or the Lord's supper; for according to the rubric and order in the Common Prayer-book, every deacon may baptize, and every minister may consecrate and administer the Lord's supper, but the bishop only may confirm.†

The Prayer after Imposition of Hands.

We make our humble supplications unto thee for these children; upon whom, after the example of thy holy apostles, we have laid our hands, to certify them, by this sign, of thy favor and gracious goodness towards them.

We desire that the practice of the apostles may not be alleged as a ground of this imposition of hands for the confirmation of children, both because the apostles did never use it in that case, as also because the Articles of the Church of England declare it to be a "corrupt imitation of the apostles' practice," Acts xxv.

We desire that imposition of hands may not be made, as here it is, a sign to certify children of God's grace and favor towards them; because this seems to speak it

---

* Discussed without result. Conceded and proposed in 1668. Applied.

† Conceded at Frankfort in 1555. Discussed in the Answer and Rejoinder without result. Applied. P. 136.

a sacrament, and is contrary to that fore-mentioned 25th Article, which saith, that "confirmation hath no visible sign appointed by God."*

The last Rubric after Confirmation.

None shall be admitted to the holy communion, until such time as he can say the Catechism, and be confirmed.

We desire that confirmation may not be made so necessary to the holy communion, as that none should be admitted to it unless they be confirmed.†

OF THE FORM OF SOLEMNIZATION OF MATRIMONY.

The man shall give the woman a ring, &c., ⸻ shall surely perform and keep the vow and covenant betwixt them made, whereof this ring given and received is a token and pledge, &c.

Seeing this ceremony of the ring in marriage is made necessary to it, and a significant sign of the vow and covenant betwixt the parties; and Romish ritualists give such reasons for the use and institution of the ring, as are either frivolous or superstitious; it is desired that this ceremony of the ring in marriage may be left indifferent, to be used or forborne.‡

The man shall say, With my body I thee worship.

This word "worship" being much altered in the use of it since this form was first drawn up, we desire some other word may be used instead of it.§

---

* Discussed without result. Conceded and proposed in 1668.
† Partially conceded and adopted.
‡ Discussed without result. Applied.
§ Proposed at Hampton Court in 1603. Conceded in 1641. Conceded in the Answer, but not adopted in the English Prayer-book. Adopted in American Prayer-books.

In the name of the Father, and of the Son, and of the Holy Ghost.

These words being only used in baptism, and here in the solemnization of matrimony, and in the absolution of the sick; we desire it may be considered, whether they should not be here omitted, lest they should seem to favor those who count matrimony a sacrament.*

Till death us depart.

This word "depart" is here improperly used.†

Rubric.

Then the minister or clerk going to the Lord's table, shall say or sing this psalm.

Next Rubric.

The psalm ended, and the man and the woman kneeling before the Lord's table, the priest standing at the table, and turning his face, &c.

Exception.

We conceive this change of place and posture mentioned in these two rubrics is needless, and therefore desire it may be omitted.‡

Collect.

Consecrated the state of matrimony to such an excellent mystery.

Exception.

Seeing the institution of marriage was before the fall, and so before the promise of Christ, as also for that the said passage in this collect seems to countenance the opinion of making matrimony a sacrament, we desire that clause may be altered or omitted.§

Rubric.

Then shall begin the communion, and after the

Exception.

This rubric doth either enforce all such as are un-

---

* Discussed without result. Not applied.
† Conceded and adopted in all Prayer-books.
‡ Discussed. Modified and proposed in 1689. Adopted in the Protestant Episcopal Prayer-book.
§ Discussed without result. Conceded and proposed in 1668. Applied.

Gospel shall be said a sermon, &c.

Last Rubric.

The new married persons the same day of their marriage must receive the holy communion.

fit for the sacrament to forbear marriage, contrary to Scripture, which approves the marriage of all men; or else compels all that marry to come to the Lord's table, though never so unprepared: and therefore we desire it may be omitted, the rather because that marriage festivals are too often accompanied with such divertisements as are unsuitable to those Christian duties, which ought to be before and follow after the receiving of that holy sacrament.*

OF THE ORDER FOR THE VISITATION OF THE SICK.

Rubric before Absolution.

Here shall the sick person make a special confession, &c., after which confession the priest shall absolve him after this sort: Our Lord Jesus Christ, &c., and by his authority committed to me, I absolve thee.

Exception.

Forasmuch as the conditions of sick persons be very various and different, the minister may not only in the exhortation, but in the prayer also be directed to apply himself to the particular condition of the person, as he shall find most suitable to the present occasion, with due regard had both to his spiritual condition and bodily weakness; and that the absolution may only be recommended to the minister to be used or omitted as he shall see occasion.

That the form of absolution be declarative and conditional, as, "I pronounce thee absolved"—instead of, "I absolve thee"—"if thou dost truly repent and believe."†

---

* Queried in 1601. Discussed without result. Modified and proposed in 1689. Adopted in the Protestant Episcopal Prayer-book.

† Proposed in 1601. Refused in the Answer. Modified and proposed in 1689. Expunged from American Prayer-books.

THE PRESBYTERIAN EXCEPTIONS. 175

OF THE COMMUNION OF THE SICK.

Rubric.

But if the sick person be not able to come to the church, and yet is desirous to receive the communion in his house, then he must give knowledge over-night, or else early in the morning, to the curate: and having a convenient place in the sick man's house, he shall there administer the holy communion.

Consider, that many sick persons, either by their ignorance or vicious life, without any evident manifestation of repentance, or by the nature of the disease disturbing their intellectuals, be unfit for receiving the sacrament. It is proposed, that the minister be not enjoined to administer the sacrament to every sick person that shall desire it, but only as he shall judge expedient.*

OF THE ORDER FOR THE BURIAL OF THE DEAD.

We desire it may be expressed in a rubric, that the prayers and exhortations here used are not for the benefit of the dead, but only for the instruction and comfort of the living.†

First Rubric.

The priest meeting the corpse at the church-stile, shall say, or else the priest and clerk shall sing, &c.

We desire that ministers may be left to use their discretion in these circumstances, and to perform the whole service in the church, if they think fit, for the preventing of those inconveniences which many times both ministers and people are exposed unto by standing in the open air.‡

The second Rubric.

When they come to the grave, the priest shall say, &c.

---

* Discussed without result. Applied.
† Applied.
‡ Ridiculed in the Answer, but adopted in the Prayer-book.*

Forasmuch as it hath pleased Almighty God, of his great mercy to take unto himself the soul of our dear brother here departed; we therefore commit his body to the ground in sure and certain hope of resurrection to eternal life.

These words cannot in truth be said of persons living and dying in open and notorious sins.*

The first Prayer.

We give thee hearty thanks for that it hath pleased thee to deliver this our brother out of the miseries of this sinful world, &c.

These words may harden the wicked, and are inconsistent with the largest rational charity.†

That we, with this our brother, and all other departed in the true faith of thy holy Name, may have our perfect consummation and bliss.

The last Prayer.

That when we depart this life, we may rest in him, as our hope is this our brother doth.

These words cannot be used with respect to those persons who have not by their actual repentance given any ground for the hope of their blessed estate.‡

OF THE THANKSGIVING OF WOMEN AFTER CHILD-BIRTH, COMMONLY CALLED CHURCHING OF WOMEN.§

Rubric.

The woman shall come unto the church, and there

In regard that the women's kneeling near the

---

* Conceded or Queried in 1641. Discussed in the Answer and Rejoinder. Conceded and proposed in 1668, and 1698. Adopted in Protestant Episcopal Prayer-book.

† See preceding note.

‡ Ibid.

§ The proposed changes were discussed with as little result as in previous instances. The office having become obsolete, is omitted, or retained in the form of an occasional Prayer and Thanksgiving.

shall kneel down in some convenient place nigh unto the place where the table stands, and the priest standing by her shall say, &c.

table is in many churches inconvenient, we desire that these words may be left out, and that the minister may perform that service either in the desk or pulpit.

Rubric.

Then the priest shall say this Psalm cxxi.

Exception.

This Psalm seems not to be so pertinent as some other, viz., as Psalm cxiii. and Psalm cxxviii.

O Lord, save this woman thy servant.
Ans. Which putteth her trust in thee.

It may fall out that a woman may come to give thanks for a child born in adultery or fornication, and therefore we desire that something may be required of her by way of profession of her humiliation, as well as of her thanksgiving.

Last Rubric.

The woman that comes to give thanks, must offer the accustomed offerings.

This may seem too like a Jewish purification, rather than a Christian thanksgiving.

The same Rubric.

And if there be a communion, it is convenient that she receive the holy communion.

We desire this may be interpreted of the duly qualified; for a scandalous sinner may come to make this thanksgiving.

Thus have we, in all humble pursuance of his majesty's most gracious endeavors for the public weal of this Church, drawn up our thoughts and desires in this weighty affair, which we humbly offer to his majesty's commissioners for their serious and grave consideration; wherein we have not the least thought of depraving or reproaching the Book of Common Prayer, but a sincere desire to contribute our endeavors towards the healing the distempers, and (as soon as may be) reconciling the minds of brethren. And inasmuch as his majesty hath in his gracious Declaration and Commission mentioned new forms to be made and suited to the several parts of worship; we have made a considerable progress therein, and shall (by God's assistance) offer them to the reverend commissioners with all convenient speed. And if the Lord shall graciously please to give a blessing to these our endeavors, we doubt not but the peace of the Church will be thereby settled, the hearts of ministers and people comforted and composed, and the great mercy of unity and stability (to the immortal honor of our most dear sovereign) bestowed upon us and our posterity after us.

APPENDIX III.

GENERAL INDEX

OF THE HISTORICAL SOURCES OF THE PRESBYTERIAN PRAYER-BOOK.

		A. D.
Emendation,	*Presbyterian,*	1661.
Preface,	*Editor.*	
Tables of Daily Psalms and Lessons,		
Tables of Proper Psalms and Lessons,	*English Reformed,*	1549.
Table of Lessons for the Lord's days.	*Church of Scotland.*	–

MORNING PRAYER.

Sentences,	*Calvin,*	1545.
Exhortation,	*Pollanus,*	1550.
Confession,	*Lasco,*	1551.
Absolution,	*Cranmer,*	1552.
Doxology in the Lord's Prayer,	*Presbyterian,*	1661.
Versicle, (Ps. lv. 15,)	*Ancient Usage,*	500.
Gloria Patri,	*Nicene.*	451.
Venite, (Ps. xcv.,)	*Ancient Usage,*	
Monthly Arrangement of Psalter,	*English Usage,*	1549.
Te Deum,	*St. Ambrose.* (?) *St. Augustine.* (?) *Hilary,*	355.
Laudate Dominum, (Ps cxlviii.,)	*Presbyterian,*	1661.
Benedictus, (Luke i. 68,)	*Ancient Usage.*	
Jubilate Deo, (Ps. c.,)	*First Revision,*	1552.
Apostles' Creed,	*Ruffinus,*	250.
Salutation	*Primitive.*	
Versicles, (Ps. li. 10, 11,)	*Ancient Usage.*	
Collect for the Day,	*Ancient Origin. English Usage,*	1549.
Collect for Peace,	*Gelasius, English Usage,*	494. 1549.

(179)

180   APPENDIX.

		A. D.
Collect for Grace,	{ *Gregory,*	590.
	Ancient Usage,	590.
Prayer for the Chief Magistrate,	{ *English Reformed,*	1545.
	English Usage,	1661.
Prayer for Ministers and People,	{ *Gelasius,*	494.
	English Usage,	1661.
Prayer for all Conditions of Men,	*Presbyterian Revision,*	1661.
General Thanksgiving,	*Presbyterian Revision,*	1661.
Prayer of St. Chrysostom,	*St. Chrysostom,*	400.
Benediction, (2 Cor. xiii. 14,)	*English Usage,*	1661.

EVENING PRAYER.

Sentences, Exhortation, &c.,	*Calvinistic Revision,*	1552.
First Versicle, (Ps. lv. 15,)	*English Usage,*	1552.
Magnificat, (Luke i. 46,)	*Ancient Usage.*	
Cantate Domino, (Ps. xcviii.,)	*English Usage,*	1552.
Nunc Dimittis, (Luke ii. 29,)	*Ancient Usage.*	
Benedic Anima, (Ps. ciii.,)	*American Usage,*	1798.
Collect for Peace,	{ *Gelasius,*	494.
	English Usage,	1549.
Collect for Grace,	*Ancient Usage,*	494.

THE LITANY.

The Litany,	{ *Apostolical Constitutions,*	300.
	Roman,	590.
	Anglo-Saxon,	900.
	Bucer,	1543.
	Cranmer,	1549.
	Amended,	1661.
	"	1798.

THE LORD'S DAY SERVICE.

Collect for Purity,	{ *Ancient.*	
	English Usage,	1549.
Ten Commandments,	{ *Calvin,*	1545.
	Pollanus,	1550.
	Cranmer,	1552.
Summary of the Law,	*American Usage,*	1798.
Collect, Epistle, and Gospel for the Day,	*Ancient Usage,*	400.
Eight Beatitudes,	*Proposed Revision,*	1698.
Gloria in Excelsis,	*Greek Church,*	300.
Nicene Creed,	*Council of Nicæa,*	451.
Collect before Sermon,	*Ancient.*	
Collect after Sermon,	*English Reformed,*	1549.
Benediction,	*Bucer,*	1545.
First Concluding Collect,	*Proposed Revision,*	1698.
Second, Third, and Fourth Concluding Collects,	*Ancient.*	
Benedictions,	*New Testament.*	

HISTORICAL INDEX OF PRAYER-BOOK. 181

THE COLLECTS FOR THE CHRISTIAN YEAR.

		A. D.
First and Second in Advent,	*English Reformed,*	1549.
Third in Advent,	*Composed,*	1661
Fourth in Advent,	*Gelasius,*	494.
Christmas.	*English Reformed,*	1549.
Sunday after Christmas,	*Altered Ancient,*	1549.
Circumcision of Christ,	*Gregory,*	590.
Epiphany,	"	"
First, Second, Third and Fifth after Epiphany.	"	"
Fourth after Epiphany,	*Altered Ancient,*	1661.
Sixth after Epiphany,	*Composed,*	1661.
Septuagesima,	*Gregory,*	590.
Sexagesima,	*Altered Gregory,*	1549.
Quinquagesima,	*English Reformed,*	1549.
Ash Wednesday,	" "	"
First in Lent,	" "	"
Second, Third, Fourth, and Fifth in Lent.	*Gregory,*	590.
Sunday next before Easter,	*Gelasius,*	494.
Good Friday, First Collect,	*Gregory,*	590.
" Second "	*Gelasius,*	494.
" Third "	*English Reformed,*	1549.
Easter Even,	*Composed,*	1661.
Easter Day,	*Gelasius,*	494.
First and Second after Easter,	*English Reformed,*	1549.
Third after Easter,	*Leo,*	483.
Fourth "	*Altered Ancient,*	1661.
Fifth "	*Gelasius,*	494.
Ascension Day,	*Gregory,*	590.
Sunday after Ascension,	*Altered Ancient,*	1661.
Whitsunday,	*Gregory,*	590.
Trinity,	"	"
First after Trinity,	*Gelasius,*	494.
Second "	*Altered Ancient,*	1661.
Third, Fourth, Fifth,	*Gregory,*	590.
Sixth, Seventh, Eighth,	*Gelasius,*	494.
Ninth, Tenth,	*Leo,*	483.
Eleventh,	*Gelasius,*	494.
Twelfth, Thirteenth, Fourteenth,	*Leo,*	483.
Fifteenth, Sixteenth,	*Gelasius,*	494.
Seventeenth,	*Gregory,*	590.
Twentieth, Twenty-first,	*Gelasius,*	494.
Twenty-second,	*Anglo-Saxon,*	900.
Twenty-third, Twenty-fourth, Twenty-fifth,	*Gregory,*	590.

THE COMMUNION SERVICE.

First Rubric,	*Directory,*	1788.
Second Rubric,	*Larger Catechism,*	1644.
Exhortations,	{ *Bucer.*	1545.
	Peter Martyr,	1552.

182 APPENDIX.

		A. D.
Rubrics before Exhortations,	*Calvinistic Revision,*	1552.
	Presbyterian Revision,	1661.
	Directory,	1788.
Prayer for Church Militant,	*Ancient.*	
	Reformed,	1549.
	Revised,	1552.
Words of Institution,	*Directory,*	1788.
Admonition,	*English Reformed,*	1549.
	Directory.	1645.
Invitation,	*English Reformed,*	1549.
	Directory,	1645.
Confession,	*Bucer,*	1545.
	Pollanus,	1550.
	Presbyterian,	1661.
Absolution,	*Altered Ancient,*	1549.
	Revised,	1552.
Comfortable Words,	*Cologne Liturgy,*	1545.
Prayer of Humble Access,	*English Reformed,*	1545.
	Presbyterian Revision,	1661.
Versicles, Preface, Tersanctus,	*Apostolic.*	
	Latin Usage,	300.
	Ante Nicene,	400.
Consecrating Prayer,	*Altered Ancient,*	1549.
	Calvinistic Revision,	1552.
	Shorter Catechism.	1661.
Breaking of the Bread,	*Calvinistic Liturgies.*	
	Directory,	1645.
	Presbyterian,	1661.
Administration of Bread and Wine,	"	"
Sentences of Scripture,	*Reformed Liturgies,*	1545.
	Book of Common Order,	1555.
Thanksgivings,	*English Reformed,*	1552.
Gloria in Excelsis,	*English Usage,*	1552.
Nunc Dimittis,	*Calvinistic Usage,*	1545.
Benediction,	*Directory,*	1788.
Rubrics,	*Confession of Faith,*	1645.

BAPTISM OF INFANTS.

First Rubric,	*Directory,*	1645.
Second Rubric,	*Westminster Catechism,*	1645.
The Gospel, Exhortation, Thanksgiving, First Prayer,	*Luther,*	1533.
	Melancthon,	1545.
	Bucer,	1551.
	Cranmer,	1552.
	Amended,	1661.
Second Prayer,	*Amended Ancient,*	1661.
Address to Parents, Questions to Parents,	*Bucer,*	1551.
	Amended,	1661.
	Directory,	1788.
Petitions,	*Luther,*	1533.
	Bucer,	1551.
	Amended,	1661.

HISTORICAL INDEX OF PRAYER-BOOK. 183

		A. D.
Words of Administration,	Our Lord.	
Words of Reception,	{ English Reformed,	1549.
	Amended,	1661.
Exhortation, }	{ Calvinistic Revision,	1552.
Lord's Prayer, }	{ Presbyterian Revision,	1661.
Thanksgiving, }		
Final Address to Parents,	{ English Reformed,	1549.
	Calvinistic Liturgies.	
Rubrics,	Confession of Faith,	1645.
Rubric concerning Guardians,	Assembly's Acts,	1787.

CATECHISM.

Rubric,	Directory,	1788.
The Lord's Prayer, }		
The Commandments, }	Shorter Catechism,	1788.
The Creed. }		
The Catechism,	Westminster Assembly,	1645.

ADMISSION TO THE LORD'S SUPPER.

Rubrics,	Directory,	1788.
Versicles, }	{ English Reformed,	1549.
Collect, }	{ Amended.	1661, 1668.
Questions to Candidate,	Amended Ancient.	
Benedictional Prayer,	Calvinistic Revision,	1552.
First Collect,	{ German,	1545.
	English,	1549.
Second Collect,	Ancient.	

BAPTISM OF ADULTS.

First Rubric,	Confession of Faith,	1645.
Second Rubric,	Directory.	1788.
Addresses, Prayers, etc.,	{ Office of Infant Baptism,	1641.
	Amended,	1661.

SOLEMNIZATION OF MARRIAGE.

First Rubric,	Directory,	1645.
Second "	"	1788.
Third "	Ancient.	
Fourth "	Directory,	1788.
	{ Bucer,	1545.
Exhortation,	{ Lasco,	1545.
	{ Cranmer,	1549.
	{ Knox,	1555.
The Espousals, }		
The Ceremony of the Ring, }	Ancient.	
The First Prayer,	Amended Ancient,	1549.

184 APPENDIX.

		A. D.
The Second Prayer,	{ Amended Ancient,	1549.
	Presbyterian Revision,	1661.
Declaration to the Witnesses,	Cologne Liturgy,	1545.
Benedictions,	Ancient.	
Homily,	English Reformed,	1549.

VISITATION OF THE SICK.

First Rubric,	Directory,	1645.
Vsrsicles, Prayers, Exhortations,	{ Amended Ancient, Presbyterian Revision,	1549. 1661.
De Profundis,	American Usage,	1798.
Benedictions,	English Reformed,	1549.
The Four Occasional Prayers,	Revision,	1661.
The Communion of the Sick,	{ Ancient. Assembly's Act,	1863.

BURIAL OF THE DEAD.

First Rubric,	Presbyterian,	1661.
First Sentence of Scripture, Second " "	} Ancient.	
Third " "	English Reformed,	1549.
Psalms, Lesson,	" "	"
The Sentences at the Grave,	{ Ancient. Luther,	1533.
The Words of Committal,	Bucer,	1552.
The Sentence after Committal,	Ancient Usage,	
The Prayers after Burial,	{ Calvinistic Revision, Knox's Liturgy,	1552. 1555.
Benediction,	Revision,	1661.
Prayer after Burial at Sea,	Manual of Worship.	

INDEX OF THE ADDITIONAL SERVICES.

The word *Compiled* will, in most instances, indicate those examples which are not afforded, in a complete form, by any ancient or modern formulary, but which the Editor has woven, after the classic models, out of such scriptural and liturgical expressions as seemed to be most suitable. The word *Ancient* indicates those which date before the Reformation, and the authors of which are unknown.

VISITATION OF MOURNERS.

Lessons,	Lutheran Liturgy.
Scripture Sentences,	{ Presbyterian Hand-book. Baptist Hand-book.
First, Second, Fourth, Fifth, Sixth Prayers,	} Compiled.
Third Prayer,	Clergyman's Companion.
Seventh Prayer,	Jeremy Taylor.

PUBLIC HUMILIATION.

		A. D.
Sentences, General Confession,	Altered English State-Services.	
Proper Psalms and Lessons,	Compiled.	
The Collect,	Ancient.	
A Prayer in Time of Pestilence,	Compiled.	
In Time of Plague,	Old English,	1552.
In Time of Drought,	Compiled.	
In time of Dearth or Famine, For Rain, For Fair Weather, In Time of War,	Old English,	1552.
In Time of Insurrections and Tumults,	John Knox.	
In Troublous Times,	Bishop A. Potter.	
For the Preservation of the Nation,	Compiled.	
For the Return of Peace, For the Restitution of all things, Concluding Prayer,	Ancient.	

PUBLIC THANKSGIVING.

Sentences, General Thanksgiving,	Amended English State-Services.	
Proper Psalms and Lessons,	Compiled.	
The Collect,	Ancient.	
Thanksgivings after Harvest,	English Occasional Offices.	
For American Independence, For the Bounties of Providence, For the Removal of Pestilence,	Compiled.	
For Deliverance from Plague, Second Example.	Old English,	1604.
For Removal of Famine,	Compiled.	
For Rain, For Fair Weather, For Plenty, For Victory,	Old English,	1604.
For any Great Public Deliverance, For Restoration of Peace at Home,	Amended Old English,	1661.
For Restoration of Peace Abroad, For Promise of Millenium,	Compiled.	

DAILY PRAYERS.

Introductory Collects, Morning and Evening Collects,	Ancient.
For the Civil Authorities, In Legislatures, In the Army,	Compiled.

APPENDIX.

		A. D.
In the Navy,	*English,*	1661.
In Schools,	*Compiled.*	
In Families,	*Ancient.*	
Concluding Collects,	*Ancient.*	

VARIOUS PRAYERS.

First Collect,	*English Reformed,*	1549.
Second "	*Calvin,*	1550.
Third "	*Compiled.*	
Fourth "	*Ancient.*	
A Confession of Original Sin,	*Calvin,*	1544.
Of Sins of the Heart,	{ *Lutheran.* *German Reformed,*	1563.
Of Thought, Word, and Deed,	*Ancient.*	
First Collect for Pardon,	*Ancient.*	
Second " "	*Old English,*	1560.
First Collect for Penitence,	" "	1560.
Second " "	*Ancient.*	
For Holy Living,	*Old English,*	1560.
For Purity,	*Ancient.*	
For Faith, For Knowledge, }	*Old English,*	1560.
For Humility, For Patience, }	*Ancient.*	
For Perseverance, For Hope, For Witness of the Holy Spirit, }	*Old English,*	1560.
Before the Communion, At the Communion }	*Ancient.*	
Before Baptism of Children,	*Reformed Dutch Liturgy.*	
For Baptized Children,	*Amended Ancient.*	
Before the Election of Elders or Deacons, For the General Assembly, }	*Compiled.*	
For the Church Universal,	*English,*	1698.
For Congress,	*Amended English,*	1661.
At the Beginning of the Day, Against Worldly Carefulness, At Night, }	*Old English,*	1560.
For Absent Friends,	*Compiled.*	
For the Sick, For the Dying, }	*Amended Ancient.*	
After Instances of Mortality,	*Clergyman's Companion.*	
After a Burial,	*Compiled.*	
On Commencing a Journey, On Commencing a Voyage, }	*Amended Ancient.*	
For Persons going to Sea, For a Person Under Affliction, }	*Protestant Episc. Prayer-book.*	
For Food, For Rain, For Fair Weather, }	*Amended Ancient.*	
Prayers in Storms at Sea,	{ *Presbyterian.* *Episcopalian.*	

HISTORICAL INDEX OF PRAYER-BOOK. 187

A. D.

Among Enemies, For Charity toward Enemies, For Prisoners, For the Wounded,	... Amended Ancient.	
For a Person Cast into Prison, For Imprisoned Malefactors, For Persons under Sentence of Death,	Irish Prayer-book,	1711.
After a Disaster in War,.............	Compiled.	
Before a Fight, Short Prayers,	Old English,	1543.
Collects in reference to Various Sacred Events and Persons,	Ancient.	
A Prayer For Christian Missions,..	English Occasional Office.	
For Christian Rulers and Nations, For the Jews, For Infidels and Heretics,	... Ancient.	
A General Prayer Containing the Duty of Every Christian,	... Old English,	1560.

VARIOUS THANKSGIVINGS.

For the Benefits of Redemption, After the Communion,	Knox's Liturgy,	1555.
After Child-birth, ...	Amended Ancient.	
After Baptism of Children,...........	Reformed Dutch.	
At the Beginning of the Day, Second Example,	...... Old English,	1560.
For the Beginning of Recovery, For Recovery of Sickness.	Protestant Episcopal.	
For Recovery of Sick or Wounded, For Supplies of Food, For Returning Rain,	Amended Ancient.	
For Deliverance from Storms,......	Compiled.	
Second Example,........................	{ Presbyterian. Episcopalian.	
For Deliverance from Enemies,......	Old English,	1604.
For Safe Return of Prisoners,......	Amended Ancient.	
For Safe Return from Sea,...........	Protestant Episcopal.	
For Safe Return from Campaign,..	Compiled.	

APPENDIX IV.

COMPARATIVE VIEW OF DIFFERENT LITURGIES.

PRIMITIVE.	MEDIEVAL.	LUTHERAN.	CALVINISTIC.	EPISCOPALIAN.	PRESBYTERIAN.
Service of Hearers, or Catechumens.	*Ordinarium Missæ.*	*Sunday Service.*	*The Lord's Day Service.*	*Ante-Communion.*	*The Lord's Day Service.*
	Versicles with Gloria.	Introit.	Psalmody.	(Morning Prayer.)	(Morning Prayer.)
Psalmody with Gloria Patri.	Confiteor, Absolutio.	Exhortation.	Ten Commandments.	The Lord's Prayer.	Collect for Purity.
	Introit, (Anthem).	Confession.	Invocation.	Collect for Purity.	Lord's Prayer.
	Kyrie Eleison.	Kyrie Eleison.	Confession.	Ten Commandments.	Ten Commandments.
Old Testament Lesson.	Gloria in Excelsis.	Gloria in Excelsis.	Absolution.	Summary of the Law.	Summary of the Law.
	Collect of the Day.	Collect of the Day.		Collect of the Day.	Collect of the Day.
	Epistle.	Epistle.		Epistle.	Epistle.
				Gloria.	
New Testament Lesson.	Gradual.	Gospel.	New Testament Lesson.	Gospel.	Beatitudes.
	Gospel.	Creeds.		(Creeds.)	Gloria in Excelsis.
	Nicene Creed.	Litany.	Sermon.		(Creeds.)
Sermon.		Sermon.	General Prayer.	Sermon.	(Litany.)
General Prayer.		Hymn.	Creed.	Prayer and Hymn.	Sermon.
Dismissal of Hearers with Benediction.		Benediction.	Psalm.	Benediction.	Prayer and Hymn.
			Benediction.		Benediction.
Service of Believers, or Eucharist.	*Canon Missæ.*	*Evangelical Mass.*	*The Lord's Supper.*	*Holy Communion.*	*The Lord's Supper.*
	Offertorium.	Salutation.	The Lord's Prayer.	Offertory.	(Collection.)
Oblation.	Oblation.	Sursum Corda.	Invocation.	Prayer for Church Militant.	Prayer for Church Militant.
Admonition.	Sursum Corda.	Preface, with Sanctus.	Creed.	The Exhortation.	Words of Institution.
Invitation.	Preface, with Sanctus.	Exhortation.	Words of Institution.	The Invitation.	Admonition.
Sursum Corda.	Prayer for the Church.	Consecration Prayer.	Exhortation.	Confession.	Invitation.
Tersanctus.	Commemoration of Dead.	The Lord's Prayer.	Consecrating Prayer.	Absolution.	Confession.
Thanksgiving.	Words of Institution.	Agnus Dei or Hymn.		Comfortable Words.	Absolution.
Consecrating Prayer.	The Lord's Prayer.			Sursum Corda.	Comfortable Words.
(Words of Institutio.)	Breaking of the Host.		Breaking of the Bread.	Preface, with Tersanctus.	Prayer of Humble Access.
	Agnus Del.			Prayer of Humble Access.	Sursum Corda.
Communion.	Priest's Prayer of Access.	Communion.	Words of Christ.	Prayer of Consecration.	Preface and Tersanctus.
	Priest's Communion.	Nunc Dimittis.	Communion.	Words of Institution.	Consecrating Prayer.
Thanksgiving.				Communion.	Breaking of the Bread.
(Lord's Prayer.)	Thanksgiving.	Thanksgiving.	Thanksgiving.	The Lord's Prayer.	Communion.
Doxology.	Post-Communion Anthem.		Nunc Dimittis.	Thanksgiving.	(The Lord's Prayer.)
Benediction.	Ite Missa est.	Benediction.	Benediction.	Gloria in Excelsis.	Thanksgiving.
	Benedicamus.			Benediction.	Hymn and Doxology.
					Benediction.

www.ingramcontent.com/pod-product-compliance
Lightning Source LLC
Chambersburg PA
CBHW020240170426
43202CB00008B/165